Suzy Tracy

Twelve Lessons in Scientific Cookery

Suzy Tracy

Twelve Lessons in Scientific Cookery

ISBN/EAN: 9783744764490

Printed in Europe, USA, Canada, Australia, Japan

Cover: Foto ©Andreas Hilbeck / pixelio.de

More available books at **www.hansebooks.com**

Scientific Cookery,

— BY —

MISS SUZY TRACY,

*GRADUATE OF MINNEAPOLIS COOKING SCHOOL
AND CHAUTAUQUA NEW YORK COOKING SCHOOL.*

PRICE SEVENTY-FIVE CENTS.

San Francisco:
H. S. Crocker Company, Printers and Stationers, 215, 217 and 219 Bush St.

1897.

PREFACE.

In presenting these pages to the consideration of the public, I do so at the earnest solicitation of many of my lady patrons who have attended my lectures, but have not always been successful in taking correct notes. I therefore put into print this pamphlet of recipes where the formula is given, followed by the explicit directions of how to put together the ingredients ; with such notes and hints as may be of value to the experimenter.

I sincerely hope the reader, especially the young housewife, may find the following pages of assistance in her household duties.

The directions are not theories but are the fruits of practical experience. They are as free from technicalities as the nature of the subject seems to permit, and the author sincerely hopes that they will prove profitable to the reader. The arrangement of the subject-matter is designed to make the book a household reference book that can be depended upon.

Respectfully,

THE AUTHOR.

INDEX.

❧ Soups ❧

There are two principal ways of making soup stock. They are known as clear stock and mixed stock. To make a clear soup we always use fresh meat and bone; the second stock being made from bones and pieces of meat left from roasts and uncooked meats.

As this latter is made from bits of meat and bone left over, no household should be without a stock-pot. Into the stock-pot should go only such meat and bone as is perfectly sweet, the smallest piece of tainted meat will destroy the soup. Stock can be cooked on the back part of the stove while other cooking is going on. It should be cooled quickly and not allowed to stand on the back part of the stove to cool slowly. Stock allowed to cool slowly becomes sour very readily.

To prepare soup bone for clear stock remove the outer skin from the meat and bone, wipe carefully with a wet cloth. (Do not put into a pan of water and wash, as the water draws out the juices, which should be kept for the soup.) Have the butcher break the bone in many pieces. In buying a soup bone buy half meat and half bone.

White stock is made from chicken and veal.

Allow one quart of water to each pound of meat and bone.

CLEAR BEEF STOCK.

Buy a shin or shank of beef having half meat and half bone (about five pounds); remove the skin; cut the bone in two-inch pieces and the meat into small pieces; add five quarts of cold water and two tea-spoonfuls of salt; let come to a boil slowly; place where it will keep just below the boiling point; simmer slowly for six or eight hours, or until the meat falls from the bone; strain and cool quickly; when cold skim off the fat. For beef broth heat the plain beef stock, season with salt, pepper and a little minced parsley, and serve. This is the simplest form of beef soup.

BEEF SOUP.

Strain the soup stock, after removing the fat, into a kettle; do not allow the sediment to pass. To four quarts of stock add one small onion cut fine, one bay leaf, one stalk of celery, two sprigs of parsley, a small bouquet of sweet herbs, ten pepper corns, and six cloves; boil gently for fifteen minutes; strain through strainer cloth. Serve as a simple beef soup.

MIXED STOCK.

Cover the trimmings and tough pieces of bone left from roasts and broils with cold water; allow one teaspoonful of salt for each gallon of water; cook slowly for about four hours; then add half an onion, six cloves, six pepper corns, two sage leaves, two sprigs of thyme, one bay leaf, two sprigs of summer savory; simmer for two hours longer; strain and cool quickly. This stock can be used in sauces or served as a simple soup, garnished with vegetables or some well-cooked tapioca.

CHICKEN STOCK.

Select a hen fowl (not as strong flavored as a rooster); singe and scrub; prepare as for roasting, omitting the stuffing; place in a kettle and cover with boiling water; cook slowly until the fowl is tender; remove from broth, cooling the broth quickly; when cold, remove the fat. The chicken can be used for salad, creamed chicken, hash or cold boiled chicken.

CHICKEN BROTH.

To one quart of chicken stock add four tablespoonfuls of boiled rice and two teaspoonfuls of minced parsley; heat boiling hot; season with salt and pepper, and serve.

BOUILLON.

Five pounds of beef, taken from the round,
Two and one-half quarts of cold water,
One level teaspoonful of salt,
One carrot,
One tablespoonful of minced onion,
One sprig of parsley,
One small stalk of celery,
Four cloves and four pepper corns.

Cut the meat into small pieces, cover with the cold water and add the salt; let come to the boiling point slowly; simmer from eight to ten hours; add the seasoning and cook one-half hour longer; strain and cool quickly; next morning remove the fat; heat scalding hot; season with salt and pepper, and serve. In making bouillon all the seasoning except salt and pepper may be omitted if preferred.

VEGETABLE SOUP.

Two quarts of beef stock,
One carrot,
One-half medium-sized yellow turnip,
Two stalks of celery,
Two pounds of cabbage,
One-fourth cupful of barley,
One onion,
Two potatoes,
Salt and pepper.

Cook the barley in one quart of water for two hours; add the stock and all the vegetables, cut fine, except the potatoes; boil gently for an hour, or until the vegetables are tender, then add the potatoes and cook fifteen minutes; season with salt and pepper.

CONSOMME.

One quart of chicken or veal stock,	Two tablespoonfuls of minced onion,
One quart of beef stock,	Two cupfuls of carrots, parsnips and yellow turnip, cut fine,
Four cloves,	
One inch piece each of mace and cinnamon,	One-half bay leaf,
	Four pepper corns,
Two eggs,	One small stalk of celery,
One sprig of parsley,	Rind and juice of half a lemon.

Brown the vegetables in bacon fat, taking care not to burn them; add them and the spices to the stock and cook slowly one and one-half hours; strain and remove the fat; break the whites and shells of the eggs into one cupful of cold water and mix thoroughly; add to the soup and let come to the boiling point; add lemon, salt and pepper; cook slowly twenty minutes; strain through strainer cloth which has been wet in cold water; reheat the soup; garnish each plate with a thin slice of lemon and three allspice berries; serve very hot.

VERMICELLI SOUP.

Two quarts of beef stock,	One cupful of vermicelli,
One teaspoonful of salt,	One-half saltspoonful of pepper.
Dash of cayenne pepper,	

Cook the vermicelli in boiling water about fifteen minutes; drain; heat the stock boiling hot; season with salt and pepper; add the vermicelli, and serve. The vermicelli may be broken or left whole, according to fancy.

MACARONI SOUP.

One quart of stock,	Two sticks of macaroni,
One teaspoonful of salt,	One-half saltspoonful of pepper.

Break the macaroni into small pieces; drop into boiling salted water and cook rapidly until the macaroni is tender; drain and allow the cold water to run over it; cut into one-fourth-inch pieces; heat the stock boiling hot; season with pepper and salt; add the macaroni, and serve.

MULLIGATAWNEY.

Fowl, three pounds,	One-half teaspoonful of pepper,
Two large onions,	Veal, three pounds,
Three stalks of celery,	One small carrot,
One tablespoonful of curry powder,	Four tablespoonfuls of butter,
	Two teaspoonfuls of salt,
Five tablespoonfuls of flour,	Five quarts of water.

Cut the veal into small pieces; dress the fowl as for roasting; put into the soup kettle; add the water; cover and let come to the boiling point; simmer for four hours, or until the fowl is tender; remove the fowl from the kettle; put butter into the saucepan; cut vegetables very fine; cook in the butter fifteen minutes; skim the vegetables out of the butter and add them to the soup; to the butter add the flour and cook until brown; then add the curry powder; add the whole to the soup, and cook for two hours; season with salt and pepper, then strain and skim; remove skin and bone from the chicken; cut into small pieces; return the soup to the soup kettle after straining; add the chicken, and simmer gently for thirty minutes: serve with boiled rice.

NOTE.—To skim soup when you cannot allow it to stand until cold. Pour the soup into a bowl just large enough to hold it; set the bowl on a plate or in another vessel and fill until it runs over; let stand two or three minutes, then slowly pour a little cold water in at one side, and the fat will run over into the plate.

TOMATO SOUP.

One quart can of tomatoes,
One tablespoonful of sugar,
Four cloves,
One tablespoonful of butter,
One tablespoonful of minced onion,
One tablespoonful of cornstarch,
One tablespoonful of minced parsley,
One pint of water,
One pint of soup stock or water, .
Four pepper corns,
Two teaspoonfuls of salt.

To the tomatoes add the water, sugar, cloves, and pepper corn; stew slowly until the tomatoes are tender; press through a strainer; remove only the seeds and skin. To the stewed and strained tomatoes add the soup stock or water. Melt the butter in a small pan, add the onion and parsley and cook until lightly browned, then add the cornstarch and cook together; slowly add one cupful of the soup, stirring until it forms a smooth sauce; add to the soup and cook fifteen minutes; season with salt and pepper, strain, and serve with croutons.

CROUTONS.

Butter and cut into one-half-inch dice a slice of stale bread one-half inch in thickness; toast until nicely browned; serve with soup.

✦ Cream Soups ✦

CREAM OF ASPARAGUS.

From a bunch of asparagus break off the tough ends, using the tops and tender parts for stewing; put the tough portions into two quarts of water and simmer gently until the water is well flavored with the asparagus; make a cream sauce of two tablespoonfuls of butter, two tablespoonfuls of flour, two cupfuls of rich milk and one level teaspoonful of salt; put the butter into a saucepan and melt; add the flour and cook together, being careful not to allow it to brown; add the milk cold, stirring constantly until it thickens; then add the water, flavored with the asparagus; season with salt and pepper, and serve.

CREAM OF CELERY.

Make a celery broth by stewing some tough bits of celery in water until the water is nicely flavored; cook together one tablespoonful of butter and two tablespoonfuls of flour; then add two cupfuls of celery broth, cold; stir until it thickens; add another cupful of the broth and a cupful of rich milk; heat to the boiling point; season with salt and pepper, and serve.

CREAM OF SALSIFY.

Cook together one tablespoonful of butter and one of flour; add two cupfuls of salsify broth, made by stewing the salsify in water until the water is well flavored; stir constantly until it makes a smooth sauce; add two more cupfuls of the broth and simmer five minutes; then add one cupful of milk and half a cupful of cream; heat boiling hot; season to taste, and serve.

CREAM OF CHICKEN.

Two tablespoonfuls of butter,	Two tablespoonfuls of flour.
One cupful of milk,	One cupful of cream.
Three cupfuls of chicken broth,	Salt, pepper and celery salt.

Cook together the butter and flour; add chicken broth, cold, stirring constantly until it thickens; add milk and cream; season to taste; heat boiling hot, and serve.

CREAM OF TOMATO, OR MOCK BISQUE.

One quart can of tomatoes,	One pint of stewed and strained
Four cloves,	tomatoes,
One tablespoonful of sugar,	One pint of water,
One tablespoonful of butter,	Four pepper corns,
One and one-half cupfuls of rich	A pinch of soda.
milk,	One tablespoonful of flour.

Stew the tomatoes, water, cloves, pepper corns, sugar and soda together until the tomatoes are tender; then strain, removing the skin and seeds; cook the butter and flour together; then add the milk cold, stirring constantly until it form a smooth sauce; add one pint of the stewed and strained tomatoes; season with pepper, salt and cayenne; heat scalding hot, and serve immediately; if allowed to stand the soup will curdle; should it curdle beat with a Dover egg-beater until smooth.

PUREE OF PEA.

One tablespoonful of butter,	Two cupfuls of white stock—
One and one-half cupfuls of	veal or chicken,
water,	Two tablespoonfuls of flour.
Two cupfuls of green peas,	

Cook the peas in the water until tender; drain and rub through a puree sieve; cook together the butter and flour; add the stock and stir until thickened; add the peas and the water in which they have been cooked; simmer five minutes; season with salt and pepper, and serve.

Note.—To make a puree of any vegetable, cook the vegetable until very tender; rub through a puree sieve, and use to thicken the soup. Always use a small quantity of cornstarch, arrow root or flour in puree to keep the vegetable from settling and to make the soup smooth.

CLAM CHOWDER.

Two dozen clams,	Six potatoes,
One-fourth pound of salt pork,	One onion,
One tablespoonful of butter,	One teaspoonful of salt,
One quart of milk,	Six crackers.
One-half teaspoonful of pepper,	

Buy the clams in the shell; scrub the shell until clean; put clams into a pan with one cupful of water and cook until the top ones open; take the clams from the shell and cut off the neck with a pair of scissors; chop the necks fine, leaving the soft part whole; save the clam broth; Pare and cut the potatoes into thin slices and soak in cold water one hour; cut the pork in small pieces and fry in a pan; add the onion, chopped fine, and cook until lightly browned; put the sliced potatoes into a kettle; strain the pork fat into it and add enough boiling water to cover the potatoes; cook until the potatoes are tender, or about ten minutes; add the clam broth and the same amount of water; add salt and pepper and clams, and lastly add the hot milk and butter; put the crackers into the tureen and pour in the chowder; serve very hot.

FISH CHOWDER.

Remove the bones from a fresh white fish; cut the fish into two-inch pieces; cover the bones with water and let simmer for fifteen minutes; proceed the same as for clam chowder, using the water in which the bones have been boiled instead of the clam juice.

❧ Fish ☙

Fish should be perfectly fresh and thoroughly cooked. In buying, select only those which have firm flesh, clear eyes and the skin and scales bright. If the fish looks limp it is not fit to use. It should be washed quickly, and not allowed to stand in the water. A little salt in the water keeps the flesh firm longer.

Clean the fish as soon as possible, washing it in salt and water; remove the scales by scraping with a small knife, beginning at the tail and working towards the head; split it down the middle and remove the entrails.

To skin a fish, cut a thin strip down the backbone, slip the knife under the skin at the lower part and slip it up through the bony part of the gills; hold the bony part and pull the skin off towards the tail; remove it from the other side in the same way.

TO BONE A FISH.

Clean the fish; then take a sharp boning knife, and, beginning at the tail, slip the knife between the bone and the flesh close to the bone; scrape away the flesh carefully; scrape the flesh away from the second set of bones and slip the knife under; treat the other side in the same way, then remove the bone, cutting away the dorsal fin.

BROILED FISH.

Clean and bone the fish; grease the broiler with a piece of salt pork to keep the fish from sticking; put fish between the broiler and broil over the coals until cooked; the thickness of the fish will determine the time.

TO BROIL IN THE OVEN.

Clean and bone the fish; grease the fish sheet with salt pork (a fish sheet is a piece of sheet iron or tin); place the fish, skin down, upon the sheet; season it with pepper and salt and brush with melted butter; then dust lightly with flour; place on the upper grate of a very hot oven and cook from twenty to thirty minutes, according to the thickness of the fish; remove from the sheet and put on a hot platter; spread with Maitre d' Hotel sauce, and serve.

BOILED FISH.

The general rule for boiled fish is to wash in cold water and wipe dry; pin the fish in a piece of strong white cotton cloth to keep it from breaking; cover with boiling water, to which one teaspoonful of salt has been added, and cook gently. Rapid boiling will break the fish. A fish weighing from four to six pounds will require thirty minutes; allow about three minutes longer for each additional pound. For boiled white fish a teaspoonful of lemon juice may be added to the water. When the fish is cooked remove from the kettle; drain well; serve on a hot platter garnished with sprigs of parsley. Serve boiled fish with Hollandaise sauce, drawn butter or egg sauce.

BAKED FISH.

Scrape and wash the fish clean; for a fish weighing from four to six pounds take three cupfuls of stale bread crumbs, moisten them with three tablespoonfuls of melted butter; add one teaspoonful of salt, one-fourth teaspoonful of pepper, one tablespoonful of minced parsley and one egg beaten light; rub the fish with salt and pepper; put the stuffing into the body of the fish and fasten together with skewers; butter the fish sheet and place the fish upon it, putting it into a baking pan; dredge the fish with pepper, salt and flour; cover the bottom of the pan with hot water; bake in a hot oven about one hour, basting every fifteen minutes; when cooked, remove the sheet from the pan and slip the fish off carefully into a hot platter; pour around it tomato or Hollandaise sauce; garnish with lemon points and sprigs of parsley.

FRIED FISH.

Fish to be fried should be cleaned, washed and dried; rub with salt and pepper; roll in flour and cornmeal (half of each); then dip in beaten egg and water (one tablespoonful of water to each egg), and roll in dry bread crumbs; fry in very hot fat; serve very hot, with Beurre Noir poured over it, and garnish with sprigs of parsley.

Any kind of fish can be fried in the same way, cutting large fish into serving pieces.

NOTE.—For temperature of fat see article "Fat for Frying."

SALT CODFISH.

Wash and soak in cold water over night; change the water and cook slowly until it comes to the boiling point; set back where it will not boil, but keep hot for about half an hour; pick over and remove all skin and bones; it is then ready to be made into different dishes.

CREAMED CODFISH.

One tablespoonful of butter,	One tablespoonful of flour,
One and one-half cupfuls of milk,	One-fourth teaspoonful of pepper.
Two cupfuls of cooked codfish,	

Cook the butter and flour together; add the milk cold, stir constantly until thickened; add the fish and pepper; simmer five minutes; serve on toast.

NOTE.—Any cold white fish may be used in place of cod. The addition of one teaspoonful of minced parsley gives variety.

FISH BALLS.

One cupful of cold cooked fish,	Two cupfuls of mashed potatoes,
One egg,	Two tablespoonfuls of milk,
Two tablespoonfuls of melted butter,	Pepper and salt.

Mix the fish and potato together; moisten with butter, milk and egg; season to taste; shape into balls and cook in hot fat three minutes.

NOTE.—If cold mashed potato is used heat the potato and add milk enough to moisten it.

ESCALLOPED FISH.

One cupful of cold cooked fish,	One tablespoonful of butter,
One tablespoonful of flour,	One cupful of milk,
One-half cupful of stale bread crumbs,	Pepper and salt.

Cook butter and flour together; add milk cold and stir until it thickens; add one-half teaspoonful of salt and one-fourth teaspoonful of pepper. Butter baking dish; put a layer of fish in the bottom, then a layer of white sauce, another layer of fish and another layer of white sauce; cover the top with the bread crumbs moistened with melted butter; bake in a moderate oven about twenty minutes, or until the crumbs are nicely browned.

❧ Oysters ❧

Oysters served on the half shell should be opened just before serving. Six, on a large plate with one-half of a lime in the center, should be served to each person.

PANNED OYSTERS.

One tablespoonful of butter,	Two dozen of oysters,
One-fourth teaspoonful of salt,	Half a saltspoonful of pepper.

Melt the butter in an omelet pan or chafing dish; add the salt and pepper and then the oysters; cook until the edges curl and the oysters become plump; serve on toast.

OYSTER STEW.

Two dozen large oysters, or three dozen small ones,	Pepper and salt, One tablespoonful of butter.
One quart of milk,	

Finger the oysters carefully and remove any pieces of shell; scald the milk in double boiler; cook the oysters in their own liquor until the edges curl; then add the milk and butter; season to taste; serve with crackers.

ESCALLOPED OYSTERS.

Moisten stale bread crumbs with melted butter, and season with salt and pepper; butter the baking dish; put a layer of bread crumbs in the bottom and then a layer of oysters, another layer of crumbs and another layer of oysters; cover the whole with the crumbs and bake in a moderate oven about twenty minutes, or until the crumbs are nicely browned.

Note.—For escalloping oysters a shallow dish or platter should be used, allowing only two layers of oysters to each dish. If more are used the upper and under layers will be overcooked while the inner ones may be undercooked.

✴ Meats ✦

BOILING.

All fresh meats to be boiled should be plunged into boiling water and allowed to boil rapidly for ten or fifteen minutes, to coagulate the albumen and thus close the pores, keeping in the juices of the meat. After the meat has boiled for ten minutes place it where it will just simmer, until tender. Meat that boils rapidly will be stringy.

HAM.

Scrub the ham with a vegetable brush until perfectly clean; then place it in a large kettle with cold water and let it come to the boiling point; simmer gently until tender—it requires about twenty minutes to the pound; let stand in the water until cold, then remove the skin; roll in fine bread crumbs, stick the fat parts with whole cloves and bake in a moderate oven about half an hour.

TONGUE.

Cook slowly in boiling water until tender—about five or six hours—then plunge into cold water and peel off the skin. For salt tongue, soak over night and cover with cold water instead of boiling water when putting on to cook.

CORNED BEEF.

Wash and cover with cold water; simmer slowly five or six hours, or until tender; let stand in the water in which it was boiled if it is to be served cold. To press corned beef, remove the bones after it is cooked and put it under a heavy weight.

NEW ENGLAND DINNER.

Six pounds of corned beef,	One small white turnip,
One pound of salt pork,	One small yellow turnip,
Two or three beets,	Six or eight medium-sized pota-
Two carrots,	toes of uniform size.

Wash and soak the corned beef and pork in cold water; put it on to boil in fresh cold water; simmer until it is tender; remove from the kettle and skim the liquor; wash and pare the turnips and carrots and cut into inch slices; cut the cabbage into quarters and wash carefully; put the carrots, turnips and cabbage into the boiling liquor and cook until tender; pare and add the potatoes half an hour before serving time; cook the beets in a separate kettle; remove the skin, cut in half-inch slices; when the vegetables are cooked, drain; put the beef and pork in the center of a large platter; serve the carrots, potatoes and turnips around the edge, with the cabbage and beets in separate dishes; the beets can be cooked the day before and covered with vinegar, serving them as pickled beets; always cook the beets in a separate kettle; the corned beef may be cooked the day before and pressed, saving the liquor for cooking the vegetables.

✄ STEWING ✄

CHICKEN STEW.

Singe and cut the chicken, at the joints, into serving pieces; cover with boiling water; simmer until tender; add one teaspoonful of salt and half a saltspoonful of pepper; after removing all the large bones put the chicken, on toast, on a large platter; cook together one tablespoonful of butter and two tablespoonfuls of flour; add one and one-half cupfuls of cold milk and stir until smooth; add the chicken broth gradually; season with pepper and salt and celery salt; pour the hot sauce over the chicken and toast, and serve. If you wish to serve dumplings with the chicken stew, ten minutes before the chicken is cooked let the liquid boil up, then put in the dumplings. When you serve dumplings omit the toast.

CHICKEN FRICASSEE.

Cut the chicken as for stew; brown in hot butter before stewing; make a brown gravy by browning the butter before adding the gravy; serve on toast

VEAL STEW.

Cut the veal into small pieces; cover with boiling water; add one-half teaspoonful of salt for each quart of water; simmer until it is tender; add four or six potatoes, cut in thick slices; cook together one tablespoonful of butter and two of flour; add one cupful of cold milk; stir until smooth; add the veal broth gradually; remove bones from veal and simmer all together for five minutes, then serve.

Beef and mutton stew are made in the same way.

For stewing, the cheapest and toughest meat is used; by long, slow cooking it becomes tender.

CURRY OF RABBIT.

Cut the rabbit into serving pieces; brown in hot butter; remove from the butter and put into a stew kettle; add one large onion, cut into slices; cook one tablespoonful of flour and one of curry powder in the butter in which the rabbit was browned; add one cupful of water or stock and stir until thickened; then add one cupful of strained tomatoes, one teaspoonful of sugar, and pepper and salt to taste; pour this over the rabbit and stew until tender; add a cupful of milk; heat boiling hot; serve with boiled rice.

❧ BROILING ❧

Broiling is the most perfect way of cooking meat and fish. There are three ways of broiling,—what is known as broiling proper, pan broiling and oven broiling.

Broiling proper is to broil directly over the coals; the fire must be hot, clear and free from smoke. For meat it must be hotter than for fish. Pan broiling is cooking upon a smoking hot griddle. Oven broiling is cooking in a very hot oven. The most delicious results are obtained by broiling steaks, chops, young chickens, squabs, etc., directly over the glowing coals. Charcoal is best for broiling, but hard wood or hard or soft coal may be used, provided it is free from smoke. The point to be remembered in broiling is to have the fire, griddle or oven hot enough to instantly sear the outer surface of the meat.

The best cuts of steak make the most delicious broils, tenderness being one of the essential qualities. It must be remembered, however, that a second-class cut of steak taken from a first-class bullock will make a much better broil than a first-class cut taken from a second-class bullock. When selecting beef see that it has a thick rim of fat, that the lean is well marbled with fat and is of a bright red color after being exposed to the air for a short time.

STEAKS.

Have steak cut thick—two inches is the proper thickness for a steak; it should never be cut less than one inch. Trim off all the suet; put between a double broiler and place it as close to the coals as possible; allow it to cook for about a minute, or until the under side is well seared, then turn and sear the other side; remove a little distance from the coals and cook from fifteen to twenty minutes, turning constantly. A steak that is broiled perfectly should be puffed out in the center and should be of a delicate pink color throughout. Serve immediately on a warm platter; garnish with sprigs of parsley or watercress.

PAN BROILING.

To pan broil a steak, have the griddle smoking hot; do not put fat of any kind on the griddle; place the steak on the griddle and press close; let it cook one minute; then, with a knife, loosen from the griddle and turn; sear the other side; reduce the heat slightly and cook from fifteen to twenty minutes, turning very frequently; do not prick the steak with a fork or the juice will escape. The steak can be easily turned with two knives by slipping one under the steak and assisting to turn with the other. Broiled steak is served as soon as taken from the fire, seasoned with pepper and salt. Maitre d' Hotel sauce is sometimes served with broiled steak.

TIME FOR BROILING STEAKS.

Steak two inches in thickness requires from fifteen to twenty minutes, one and one-half inches from twelve to fifteen minutes and one inch from eight to ten minutes.

LAMB AND MUTTON CHOPS.

Remove the outer skin and all the suet from the chops; broil over the coals or on a hot griddle; serve with tomato sauce and season with salt and pepper; garnish with parsley.

NOTE.—Before cooking lamb or mutton always remove the skin. It is in the skin that the disagreeable flavor exists.

✤ ROASTING ✤

Roasting and baking are synonymous terms. We speak of roasting meats and baking bread, yet we use the same oven for both. Roasting formerly meant to place the meat on a spit before the open fire, turn it frequently and baste constantly to keep from burning. Roasting to-day means to bake in a hot oven.

ROAST BEEF.

There are seven prime ribs in a bullock. Any of them will make a first-class roast of beef. Do not have the ribs removed, but have them cut in two-inch pieces up to the thick muscle; cut these pieces of bone off, to be braised and served as short ribs of beef; place the cut surface of the roast on a smoking hot griddle and press closely; let cook for two or three minutes, or until it is nicely seared; turn and sear the other side; set the roast, resting upon the edges of the ribs, on a rack in a dripping pan; put into an oven hot enough to bake bread, and let cook; *do not* season the meat and *do not* put water in the pan; when the oven is at the proper temperature you will hear a gentle sputtering when the oven door is opened—if smoke issues from the oven it is too hot—if you do not hear a gentle sputtering increase the temperature. The time required for roasting depends upon the thickness of the roast; fifteen minutes is allowed for each inch in thickness; a roast four inches in thickness will cook rare in one hour; measure across the thickest part of a roast. A rump roast is seared in the same way and placed upon a rack in a hot oven; allow fifteen minutes to the pound.

YORKSHIRE PUDDING.

Two-thirds of a cupful of flour,   One pint of milk,
Three eggs,   One teaspoonful of salt.

Sift the flour and measure; add the salt; separate the eggs and add the yolks, unbeaten, to the flour; add a little of the milk and mix to a smooth paste; add the rest of the milk gradually; beat whites of the eggs to a stiff froth and stir into the batter; pour into the roasting pan forty-five minutes before the roast is cooked; serve hot with the roast of beef; if the roast is very fat pour some of the fat from the pan before putting in the pudding.

BRAISED BEEF OR POT ROAST.

Six or eight pounds of chuck roast; trim and rub with pepper and salt; cut a large onion into dice and brown in salt pork fat; put the roast into a braising pan; pour over it one quart of boiling water; add the onion; cover closely and cook in a moderate oven about four hours, turning after two hours, and add more water as it evaporates, so as to have three cups of gravy; when tender take up the meat; skim off the fat from the gravy and thicken with a tablespoonful of flour wet in a little cold water and strained into the gravy; season with pepper and salt and a little lemon juice.

VEAL HEART.

Remove the tough membranes and soak in cold water and salt one hour; wipe and stuff with stale bread crumbs seasoned with salt and pepper and moistened with melted butter; rub the heart with salt, pepper and dredge with flour; fry brown in a pan with a little fat salt pork; place in braising kettle; add one pint of water, one teaspoonful of minced onion, sprig of parsley, three cloves, three pepper corns, one small carrot cut fine; cover tightly and cook two hours in a moderately hot oven; turn three or four times while baking.

ROAST LAMB OR MUTTON.

Remove the skin from a leg of lamb or mutton; sear the cut surfaces on a hot griddle; place on a rack in a roasting pan in a hot oven. A leg of lamb will roast in one hour and a quarter, while it requires one hour and three-quarters to roast a medium-sized leg of mutton.

ROAST VEAL.

Veal being a dry meat, requires basting to keep it moist and to enrichen it; rub the veal with sugar, salt and pepper, using one-half as much sugar as salt; place upon rack in roasting pan and let cook in a hot oven until nicely browned, then baste with a thin gravy made from one tablespoonful of butter, one of flour and two cupfuls of stock or water; season with pepper and salt; baste every fifteen minutes; veal requires longer cooking than either beef or mutton; a five-pound roast will cook in two and one-half hours.

PORK.

Fresh pork is seasoned with pepper, salt and sugar. Roast and baste the same as veal.

✢ Poultry ✢

TO DRAW POULTRY.

All poultry should be dressed as soon as killed; the feathers come out more easily while the fowl is warm; strip them off towards the head; remove the pinfeathers with a knife; singe the hairs by holding it over the gas jet or a piece of lighted paper; cut off the head; turn the skin back and cut off the neck close to the body; remove the windpipe and crop; to remove the feet, cut the skin just below the leg joint; break the joint; with a skewer pull out the tendons; cut away the oil bag in the tail; make an incision under the side bone near the tail large enough to insert two fingers; slip the fingers around the entrails, separating the membrane; when everything is loosened, get the fingers around the heart and pull out the entrails; then take out the lungs and kidneys; when everything is removed hold the fowl under the faucet and rinse well, then wipe dry.

TO CLEAN GIBLETS.

Remove the outside sack from the heart; cut open and press out the clot of blood; cut off the gall bladder from the liver, being careful not to break it, and cut away any discolored part of the liver; open the thick part of the gizzard and take out the inner sack without breaking; wash giblets and put into cold water; simmer until tender; cook the neck with the giblets.

TO TRUSS POULTRY.

Draw the thighs up close to the body and pass a skewer through the thigh and into the body and out through the other thigh; pass another skewer through the wings, fastening them close to the body; fold the skin at the neck over and pin it to the back with a skewer; cross the legs over the tail and tie with a stout twine, leaving two long ends; pass the twine around the tail, bring it up, crossing in front and passing around the skewer in the thighs; cross in the back and fasten around the skewer through the wings, and tie firmly.

ROAST TURKEY.

Singe, draw, wash and wipe; stuff the body and neck with stale bread crumbs moistened with melted butter and seasoned with pepper, salt and celery salt; truss and rub with butter; lay the turkey, breast down, on the rack in the roasting pan; put into a hot oven and cook until the back of the turkey is nicely browned, then turn it over and brown breast; pour one pint of water into the pan after the turkey is browned; baste every fifteen minutes, or whenever the skin becomes very dry;

allow twenty-five minutes to the pound for roasting; if the turkey browns too rapidly cover the breast with a heavy paper well buttered. Oysters or chopped celery may be added to the stuffing if desired.

ROAST CHICKEN.

Prepare the same as roast turkey; allow twenty minutes to the pound for roasting.

❧ Frying ❧

Frying is cooking in hot fat deep enough to entirely cover the articles to be cooked. When food is properly fried the fat is hot enough to instantly sear the outer surface and thus prevent it soaking into the food. All food to be fried should be thoroughly dried; if water should drop into the hot fat it would cause the fat to boil over, and there is danger of it taking fire and causing great trouble. Food that does not contain sufficient albumen to form a coating on the outside as soon as immersed into the hot fat should be rolled in crumbs, then in egg and again in crumbs to form a grease-proof covering. A frying basket, or a wire basket with a long handle, is very convenient for frying purposes. In many cook books we read, "heat the fat smoking hot." That depends entirely upon the kind of fat you are using; lard will smoke at a much lower temperature than oil. When fat smokes it loses some of its browning properties; never let fat heat without putting a small piece of raw potato into it. As soon as the potato begins to brown drop in a fresh piece of potato; if it browns in one minute the fat is hot enough to fry potatoes and dough mixtures. For such food as we roll in bread crumbs and egg the fat should be hot enough to brown a bit of bread in forty seconds.

The best fat for frying purposes is a mixture of suet and oil, as both these fats can be heated to a much higher temperature without smoking than lard, and are more healthful. Olive oil is the purest fat for frying, but is too expensive for general use.

For frying the same fat can be used several times if properly cared for. The most delicate croquettes can be fried in the same fat with fish and not be marred in flavor. When frying several different kinds of food at the same time, begin with potatoes, then dough mixtures and lastly articles rolled in crumbs.

When finished with the fat drop three or four slices of raw potato into it; cool slightly, and strain through a fine strainer or a strainer cloth.

FRENCH FRIED POTATOES.

Pare the potatoes and cut into strips one-half inch in thickness; let stand in cold water one hour; heat the fat hot enough to brown a thin slice of potato in one minute; wipe the potatoes; put into the frying basket and lower into the hot fat; do not put a large quantity of potatoes in at one time, as they will lower the temperature of the fat and the potatoes will be soggy and greasy. When the potatoes are nicely browned lift from the fat and shake free from grease; turn onto a piece of cheese cloth to absorb the fat; dust lightly with salt, and serve immediately. French fried potatoes should be crisp and mealy. If they stand they become soggy.

SARATOGA CHIPS.

Pare the potatoes and slice very thin; let stand in cold water two or three hours; wipe dry; fry in fat hot enough to brown in one minute; when nicely browned remove the basket and shake well; turn chips onto cheese cloth or soft paper; dust well with salt.

LAMB CHOPS BREADED.

Trim the chops and remove the skin; season with salt and pepper; roll in fine bread crumbs; dip in beaten egg and water; add table-spoonful of water to each egg, and roll in bread crumbs; fry in hot fat. For a chop one inch in thickness it will require six minutes to cook rare and from eight to ten to cook well done.

FRIED CHICKEN.

Cut the chicken into ten pieces; season with pepper and salt; roll in fine bread crumbs; dip in beaten egg and water; roll in crumbs, and fry in fat hot enough to brown a piece of bread in one minute. A young chicken will cook in ten minutes. Serve with sauce tartare or cream sauce; garnish the dish with sprigs of parsley.

NOTE.—For fried fish see article on Fish.

CROQUETTES.

In making croquettes the material must be chopped fine, well mixed, and seasoned delicately. The shaping of croquettes can be readily acquired by a little practice and care. They are formed into cone, ball and cylindrical shapes.

To Shape.—Take a tablespoonful of the mixture; roll gently between the hands into a ball; have a board well sprinkled with fine dry bread crumbs and roll the croquette very gently on this into shape; dip into beaten egg, to which one tablespoonful of water has been added; water added to the egg makes a more elastic coating than egg alone; after dipping the croquette into the egg roll again in the bread crumbs and then fry in fat hot enough to brown a piece of bread in forty seconds; cook until nicely browned—it will require about two minutes; take up and lay on cheese cloth or soft brown paper.

CHICKEN CROQUETTES.

One pint of cooked chicken, chopped fine,
Two tablespoonfuls of butter,
Two tablespoonfuls of flour,
One cupful of cream,

One teaspoonful of minced parsley,
Pepper and salt to taste.
One teaspoonful of lemon juice,
One teaspoonful of minced onion.

Cook together the butter and flour; add the cream, and stir constantly until it thickens; season the chicken with pepper, salt, onion, lemon juice and parsley; add to the white sauce and mix thoroughly; spread on a buttered plate and set away to cool; when cold shape into croquettes; roll in bread crumbs, dip in egg, and roll again in crumbs, and fry in hot fat; drain on cheese cloth, and serve garnished with lemon points and sprigs of parsley.

SWEETBREAD CROQUETTES.

Two sweetbreads,
One tablespoonful of butter,
Two tablespoonfuls of flour,

One cup of cream,
One teaspoonful of lemon juice,
Pepper and salt to taste.

Cover the sweetbreads with cold water and salt; let stand two or three hours; cover with boiling water; add lemon juice and cook until tender; remove the tubes and membranes, and, with a silver fork, separate into small pieces; cook together the butter and flour; add the cream or rich milk and cook until thickened; add the sweetbreads; season to taste; spread on a buttered plate and set aside to cool; shape into croquettes; roll in fine bread crumbs; dip in egg and roll in crumbs again; fry in hot fat until nicely browned.

ROYAL CROQUETTES.

Royal croquettes are made by using half chicken and half sweetbreads.

POTATO CROQUETTES.

Six medium-sized potatoes,
One tablespoonful of butter,
Salt and pepper to taste,
Two-thirds of a cupful of milk,

Whites of two eggs,
One tablespoonful of minced parsley.

Pare, boil and mash potatoes; add the butter, milk and seasonings; let cool slightly, then shape; roll in crumbs, egg and crumbs, and fry.

RICE CROQUETTES.

One and one-half cupfuls of boiled rice,
Three-fourths of a cupful of milk,

Half a teaspoonful of salt,
Two eggs,
One tablespoonful of sugar,
One tablespoonful of butter.

Cover the rice with the milk; add the sugar, butter and salt; let boil three minutes; add the eggs, well beaten, and cook one minute; then take off and cool; when cold, shape, roll in crumbs, egg and crumbs; fry, and serve very hot.

OTHER CROQUETTES.

Mutton, veal, lamb, beef or any kind of cooked meat or fish may be substituted in place of chicken, and prepared in the same way; or, take one cupful of finely chopped meat and add to it one-half cupful of stale bread crumbs; moisten with one-third cupful of cream and the white of one egg; season with pepper, salt and a little onion juice; drop by spoonful into hot fat; fry until nicely browned.

FRITTER BATTER.

One cupful of flour,
Two tablespoonfuls of sugar,
One teaspoonful of baking powder,
One saltspoonful of salt,
One egg,
One-third of a cupful of milk.

Mix the flour, sugar, salt and baking powder together; add the egg, beaten light, and the milk; beat until light and smooth; drop by spoonful into very hot fat; sprinkle with sugar, and serve with maple syrup or lemon sauce.

APPLE FRITTERS.

Pare and core two large tart apples; cut into slices about one-third of an inch in thickness; drop into the fritter batter and fry about five or six minutes in very hot deep fat; serve hot with lemon sauce.

FRUIT FRITTERS.

Bananas, oranges, pineapple, peaches, etc., are used for fritters; cut into small pieces or slices and add to the fritter batter; fry in deep fat heated very hot.

CHICKEN FRITTERS.

Cut cold boiled or roast chicken into small pieces; season with salt, pepper and a tablespoonful of lemon juice for each pint of chicken; make a batter as for "Batter Fritters," omitting the sugar; stir the chicken into the batter; drop by spoonful into very hot fat; drain and serve immediately; any tender meat may be substituted for chicken.

OYSTER FRITTERS.

Prepare the fritter batter, omitting the sugar; for large oysters drain and dip into the batter, and fry in very hot fat; if the oysters are small drain and add one cupful of oysters to one cupful of batter; drop by spoonfuls in hot fat and fry until nicely browned; drain on cheese cloth or soft paper, and serve hot.

FRIED MUSH.

Cut cold mush into slices three quarters of an inch in thickness; roll in cornmeal and flour (equal parts); dip in beaten egg, to which one tablespoonful of cold water has been added; roll in cornmeal and flour and fry in hot fat; drain on cheese cloth, and serve hot.

CRULLERS.

One-fourth of a cupful of butter,	Two teaspoonfuls of baking powder,
One cupful of sugar,	
Two cupfuls of flour,	One cupful of milk,
One-half teaspoonful of nutmeg,	Three drops of almond extract.
Two eggs,	

Cream the butter; add the sugar and egg yolks and cream together; add the flour and milk alternately; sift the baking powder in with the flour; beat the whites of the eggs stiff and add before the last cup of flour; also the flavorings; roll very thin; cut into shape; fry in deep fat heated very hot; cook until nicely browned; roll in powdered sugar and cinnamon.

DOUGHNUTS.

Three eggs,	Two level teaspoonfuls of salt,
Three cupfuls of sugar,	One teaspoonful of ginger,
One teaspoonful of nutmeg,	Six teaspoonfuls of baking powder,
Three cupfuls of milk,	
One large tablespoonful of butter,	Flour enough to make a stiff batter or very soft dough.

Beat the eggs until creamy; add the sugar and beat together; add the butter, melted, and the salt, ginger and nutmeg; beat well; sift the baking powder with three cups of flour; add the milk and flour alternately and beat well together; then add enough more flour to make a very stiff batter; beat thoroughly, but do not knead; sprinkle the board well with flour; roll into a sheet about one-half inch in thickness; cut into shape and fry in very hot fat; cut all the doughnuts before frying, as the frying will require your full attention.

⇥ Sautéing ↢

Sautéing is cooking food in a small quantity of fat. Butter, when clarified, is the most satisfactory for some things, as it browns nicely and gives a delicious flavor to the food, but lard or drippings may be used.

CLARIFIED BUTTER.

To clarify butter, let it boil gently for about a minute—the salt will settle to the bottom; the scum which rises to the top should be skimmed off, leaving the oil clear.

MUSH.

Cut cold mush into thin slices; cook on a griddle buttered with clarified butter until nicely browned.

FRIED APPLES.

Cut tart apples in thin slices; dust lightly with flour, and fry in clarified butter in a spider until nicely browned; serve with liver, breakfast bacon or pork chops.

VEAL CUTLETS.

Rub the chops with salt, sugar and pepper; dredge with flour; heat one tablespoonful of clarified butter or drippings in the spider; brown the chops nicely on both sides; add two tablespoonfuls of water; cover the spider closely and let simmer ten minutes; serve on a hot platter; add one-fourth of a cupful of sweet milk to the gravy in the spider, and serve with the chops.

PORK CHOPS.

Season and cook the same as veal cutlets; veal and pork require long and thorough cooking.

HAMBURG STEAKS.

One pound of round steak chopped very fine; one tablespoonful of minced onion; pepper and salt to taste; mix the meat and seasonings thoroughly together; shape into cakes about three-fourths of an inch in thickness; grease the griddle or spider well; brown nicely on both sides; cook about five minutes, and serve.

CALF'S LIVER.

Cut in slices one-half inch in thickness; dust with pepper and salt and roll in flour; cook in bacon fat until nicely browned; serve with breakfast bacon or fried apples, or cover the liver with boiling water and let stand five minutes; season with pepper and salt; roll in flour and fry in bacon fat or clarified butter.

⇥ Salads ⇤

Salads, to be palatable, should always be crisp and fresh and served icy cold. It is upon its crispness and the proper mingling and selection of ingredients that its success depends; when lettuce is to be used it must be washed carefully, taking care not to break the leaves. The large dark leaves are not nice for salad. Of celery only the white, crisp parts are used, the green, tough parts being utilized for soups and stews. All fresh vegetables to be used for salad should stand in ice water until just before serving time. Vegetable salads are served after the meat course at dinner—a rich salad, such as lobster, chicken, sweet-bread, etc., is out of place at a heavy meal. These latter are best served at lunches or suppers. In arranging a salad on a dish or in a bowl handle it very lightly; do not press it into form. The garnishings should be of the freshest and crispest kind.

MAYONNAISE DRESSING.

Yolks of two eggs,
One pint of olive oil,

Juice of one lemon, or one-third
of a cupful of vinegar.

Place the oil and eggs in the refrigerator some time before using them. Put the yolks of the eggs into a cup just large enough to take the Dover egg-beater; beat the eggs until creamy; add a few drops of oil at a time and beat together until it thickens, then the oil can be added more rapidly; when it gets so thick that the beater turns hard add a tablespoonful of lemon juice or vinegar; add more oil and lemon juice until the oil is all used; when all the oil and vinegar are added the dressing should be thick; the dressing is seasoned according to the salad it is to be served with. The addition of a cupful of whipped cream after the seasonings are added makes a great improvement.

FRENCH DRESSING.

One tablespoonful of sharp vinegar,
Three tablespoonfuls of olive oil,

One fourth of a teaspoonful of salt,
One-half saltspoonful of pepper.

Mix the vinegar, salt, pepper and oil together and beat with a fork until the oil and vinegar unite. This dressing can be made at the table, and the salad dressed just before serving.

COOKED MAYONNAISE DRESSING.

Four egg yolks and one whole
egg.

Six tablespoonfuls of vinegar,
One generous teaspoonful of butter.

Heat the vinegar scalding hot; beat the eggs until creamy; pour the hot vinegar over the beaten eggs; cook over boiling water, stirring constantly until it thickens, then add the butter; season according to the salad to be served.

CREAM DRESSING.

One tablespoonful of butter,
Two tablespoonfuls of flour,
One-half of a cupful of cream,

One cupful of rich milk,
Four tablespoonfuls of vinegar or
lemon juice.

Melt the butter; add flour and cook together; add milk and stir until thickened; add gradually the vinegar and when cold stir in the cream.

CHICKEN SALAD.

Remove the skin and bone from a cold boiled or roast chicken; cut into half-inch dice; to one quart of diced chicken add two tablespoonfuls of lemon juice, one-half teaspoonful of salt and one-half saltspoonful of pepper; let stand in a cold place for two or three hours; cut into half-inch dice enough tender white celery to make three cupfuls; mix the chicken and celery together; season one cupful of mayonnaise dressing with one-half teaspoonful of dry mustard, one-half teaspoonful of salt, one-half saltspoonful of white pepper and a dash of cayenne; mix the seasonings together and add to the dressing; then add one-half cupful of whipped cream; mix one-half of the dressing with the chicken and celery; arrange in a salad bowl and pour the remainder of the dressing on top; garnish the dish with crisp bits of celery or white celery leaves.

Equal parts of chicken and sweetbread, or chicken and veal mixed with celery make a nice salad.

SWEETBREAD SALAD.

Cover the sweetbread with cold water; add one teaspoonful of salt and stand two or three hours; drain; cover with boiling water; add one teaspoonful of lemon juice; cook until tender; drain; drop into cold water and let stand until cold; remove the membranes and pull apart with a silver fork into small pieces; mix two cupfuls of sweetbreads, two tablespoonfuls of vinegar, one-half teaspoonful of salt and half a saltspoonful of pepper together; let stand on the ice for one hour; cut into dice cucumbers enough to make two cupfuls; let stand in ice water one hour. Season one-half cupful of mayonnaise with one-fourth of a teaspoonful of salt; mix half the dressing with the sweetbreads and cucumbers; arrange in salad bowl, and pour the remainder of the dressing on top; serve immediately.

LOBSTER SALAD.

Cut the lobster into dice; season with salt, pepper and lemon juice, the same as chicken; let stand an hour; separate and wash carefully the leaves from a crisp head of lettuce; let stand in ice water for half an hour; at serving time shake free from water; arrange two or three leaves together in the form of a nest, and arrange the nests on a large dish or individual dishes; season the mayonnaise to taste with a mixture of one teaspoonful of mustard, one teaspoonful of salt and a fourth of a teaspoonful of mixed pepper; mix one-half the dressing with the lobster; put a tablespoonful into each shell and a teaspoonful of dressing on top.

Another way of serving lobster salad is to tear the lettuce into large pieces and mix with the lobster, using one-third as much lettuce as lobster, garnishing the dish with the whole leaves.

SHRIMP SALAD.

Prepare and serve shrimps the same as lobster; the shrimps may be left whole or cut into small pieces.

Crab salad is also prepared in the same way.

FISH SALADS.

All kinds of cold cooked fish can be used for salads. Dress with a French or mayonnaise dressing, season to taste, and serve with lettuce leaves.

MEAT SALAD.

One pint of cold meat cut in thin slices and then cut into small pieces; to the French dressing add one tablespoonful of minced parsley and one teaspoonful of onion juice; put a layer of meat in the salad bowl; pour on some dressing, another layer of meat, and so on until all the meat and dressing is used; let stand on the ice two hours; garnish the dish with sprigs of parsley, and serve. Any kind of tender meat may be used.

TOMATO SALAD.

Drop six medium-sized tomatoes into boiling water; let stand two or three minutes; remove the skin; cut off about one-fourth of each tomato; with a sharp knife cut the pulp loose from the sides and scoop out the center; fill each shell with chipped ice and stand in the refrigerator for two or three hours; cut pulp and the upper part of the tomato into dice; drain; season two tablespoonfuls of mayonnaise dressing with one-fourth teaspoonful of salt; mix the mayonnaise and the diced tomatoes together; empty the tomato cups; fill with the salad and set on a lettuce leaf, or garnish the plate with nasturtium leaves.

Tomato salad may also be served without the cups.

POTATO SALAD.

Six medium-sized potatoes,
Four tablespoonfuls of cooked mayonnaise,
One tablespoonful of minced parsley,
One tablespoonful of minced onion,
One teaspoonful of dry mustard,
Two teaspoonfuls of salt,
One-fourth of a teaspoonful of white pepper,
Dash of cayenne,
Sweet cream.

Pare and cover the potatoes with boiling water; add one teaspoonful of salt; boil slowly until tender; drain; remove the cover and shake over the fire until the potatoes are dry; when cool enough to handle cut into thin slices; mix the pepper, salt, and mustard together; add to the cooked mayonnaise and mix until smooth, then add onion and parsley; slowly add sweet cream enough to make it the consistency of thin cream; put a layer of potatoes in the salad bowl; cover with the

dressing, then another layer of potatoes and more dressing until
the bowl is filled; pour the remainder of the dressing over the potatoes
and set in a cold place for two or three hours; garnish with sprigs of
parsley.

BEET SALAD.

Boil beets; remove skins and cut into dice; season with salt and
pepper; mix with cream dressing; garnish with sprigs of parsley, and
serve.

ASPARAGUS SALAD.

Boil three bunches of asparagus in boiling salted water until tender;
when cold cut off the tender parts; mix with a cream dressing, seasoned with pepper and salt, or serve six stalks with one teaspoonful of
mayonnaise to each person.

CABBAGE SALAD.

One small head of cabbage,	One-half of a teaspoonful of salt,
One-half of a cupful of cooked mayonnaise dressing,	One-half of a saltspoonful of pepper, One-half of a cupful of sweet cream.
Two tablespoonfuls of sugar,	

Divide the cabbage in four parts; wash well in cold water; take off
all the wilted leaves and cut out the tough parts from the center; shred
the cabbage very fine with a sharp knife and throw into cold water
until crisp; mix the salt, sugar and pepper together and then mix into
the dressing; add the cream gradually; shake off all the water from the
cabbage; mix with the dressing, and serve. Hard boiled eggs,
chopped fine, may be added to the salad if desired.

LETTUCE SALAD.

Break off all the leaves carefully from a head of lettuce; wash and
throw into ice water for one or two hours; then shake off all the water;
dress with French dressing, and serve. If the leaves are very large
tear into pieces.

CELERY SALAD.

Wash and cut the celery into strips; let stand in ice water for half
an hour; cut into pieces about an inch long and dress with mayonnaise
dressing, seasoned to taste with pepper and salt and mustard; arrange
in the salad bowl and garnish with choice bits of celery.

APPLE SALAD.

Three tart apples,	Six tablespoonfuls of whipped cream,
One-half pound of English wal-nuts,	One tablespoonful of sugar,
One tablespoonful of cooked mayonnaise dressing,	One-half saltspoonful of salt.

Pare, core, quarter and slice very thin the apples; chop the walnuts fine; add the sugar, salt and cream to the dressing; mix the apples and nuts and add the dressing; serve immediately.

BANANA SALAD.

Six bananas,	Juice of two large lemons,
One cupful of sugar,	One-fourth cupful of water.

Cook the sugar and water together for five minutes; when cold add the lemon juice; slice six bananas very thin into the salad bowl; pour over them the syrup and let stand one or two hours before serving.

FRUIT SALAD.

One-half dozen oranges,	One-half pound of white grapes,
Three bananas,	Juice of one lemon,
Quarter of a box of gelatine,	Powdered sugar,
Quarter of a package of cocoa- nut,	One-eighth of a pound of can- died cherries.
Half a cupful of sugar,	

Skin and seed the grapes; take the juice and pulp of the oranges, removing the seeds and membrane; peel and slice the bananas very thin; cover the gelatine with cold water and let stand half an hour; add half a cupful of boiling water and half a cupful of sugar; stir until dissolved; add the orange and lemon juice; put a layer of bananas in the bottom of individual dishes, then add the grapes and orange pulp; dredge well with the powdered sugar; pour the gelatine mixture around the fruit; cover the top with cocoanut and stick about pieces of candied cherries; place on ice until stiff enough to serve.

✦ Meat *and* Fish Sauces ✦

WHITE SAUCE.

Cook together one tablespoonful of butter and one of flour; add one cupful of rich milk; stir until smooth; season with pepper and salt.

BROWN SAUCE.

Cook one tablespoonful of butter until it browns; add two tablespoonfuls of flour and cook together until a dark brown; add one cupful of soup stock and stir until it thickens; season with pepper and salt.

HORSERADISH SAUCE.

Two tablespoonfuls of butter,	Four tablespoonfuls of horseradish,
One tablespoonful of flour,	One tablespoonful of chopped parsley,
Two cupfuls of stock,	Juice of one lemon,
Pepper and salt to taste,	One tablespoonful of sugar.

Cook the butter and flour together; add the stock and stir until it boils; add the horseradish, sugar, pepper and salt; let it boil for one minute; remove from the fire and add lemon juice and parsley. This is a nice sauce for roast veal.

MUSHROOM SAUCE.

Four tablespoonfuls of butter,	One can of mushrooms,
Two tablespoonfuls of flour,	Pepper and salt.
Two cupfuls of stock,	

Cook the butter and flour together until a dark brown; add the stock and stir until it boils, then add the liquor from the mushrooms and let the mushrooms simmer five minutes; season and serve. This is to be served with roast or braised beef.

BEURRÉ NOIR—(MISS PARLOÁ).

Two tablespoonfuls of butter,	One tablespoonful of minced parsley,
One tablespoonful of vinegar,	One teaspoonful of lemon juice,
One-half teaspoonful of salt,	One quarter teaspoonful of pepper.

Cook the butter in a saucepan until it boils; add the parsley and then the other ingredients and boil up once. This sauce to be poured over fried or boiled fish before sending to the table.

TOMATO SAUCE.

One tablespoonful of butter,	One tablespoonful of flour,
One cupful of stewed and strained tomatoes,	One tablespoonful minced onion,
	Salt and pepper.

Fry the onion in the butter until a light brown; add the flour and cook together, then the tomatoes, and stir until thickened; season with pepper and salt.

HOLLANDAISE SAUCE.

One-half cupful of butter,	Juice of half a lemon,
Yolks of two eggs,	Few grains of cayenne.
One-half cupful of boiling water,	

Cream the butter; add the eggs and cream together; add seasonings, and then the boiling water; cook in double boiler until creamy, then add lemon juice.

BUTTER SAUCE.

Two cupfuls of boiling water,	Two tablespoonfuls of flour,
One-half cupful of butter,	One tablespoonful of lemon juice.
Dash of cayenne,	

Cream the butter, add the flour and beat together; add gradually the boiling water, stirring constantly; let come to a boil; add lemon juice and pepper, and serve.

OYSTER SAUCE.

One-third of a cupful of butter,	Juice of half a lemon,
One tablespoonful of flour,	Pepper and salt and a dash of
One pint of oysters,	cayenne.

Cream the butter; add the flour and beat together; cook the oysters in their own liquor until they boil; skim out the oysters and add enough water to the liquor to make one pint; add to the butter and flour and cook until it thickens, then add the oysters and seasonings.

SAUCE TARTARE.

To one pint of mayonnaise dressing add one teaspoonful each of chopped pickles, capers, olives, parsley and onion juice; season with one-half teaspoonful of mustard, one teaspoonful of salt, one-fourth of a saltspoonful of pepper and a dash of cayenne; serve with fried or broiled fish or fish balls.

CHAMPAGNE SAUCE.

Two tablespoonfuls of butter,	One tablespoonful of flour,
One cupful of rich stock,	One-half cupful of champagne.
Pepper and salt,	

Cook the butter and flour together until a dark brown; add the stock and stir until smooth; season with salt and pepper; remove from the fire, and add the champagne.

⇥ Vegetables ⇤

All green vegetables must be cooked in freshly boiled salted water; allow one teaspoonful of salt for every quart of water. The younger the vegetable the more quickly it will cook.

POTATOES.

Nearly every housekeeper fancies she can cook a potato, and yet we have so many soggy and poor-flavored potatoes brought to our tables. The potato is composed chiefly of starch and water. When subjected to heat the starch cells burst and the potato becomes tender. If removed from the water or oven as soon as the starch is set free the potato will be mealy and dry, but if allowed to cook longer the starch will absorb the moisture and the potato be soggy.

BOILED POTATOES.

If cooking new potatoes boil them in their jackets; old potatoes, scrub, pare and let stand in cold water two or three hours to freshen them; cover with boiling water, to which a teaspoonful of salt has been added, and boil gently from twenty to thirty minutes; medium-sized potatoes will require thirty minutes; rapid boiling will break the potatoes; when cooked drain off every drop of water; remove the cover and shake the saucepan over the fire until the potatoes are dry and mealy; serve immediately. The potatoes should be put on to boil just one-half hour before they are to be served. If they must stand, set the saucepan on the back part of the stove and cover with a towel until serving time. The towel will absorb the moisture.

MASHED POTATOES.

Boil six medium-sized potatoes; drain and shake over the fire; mash fine; add one teaspoonful of salt and one level tablespoonful of butter and beat well; heat a quarter of a cupful of milk; pour the hot milk over the potatoes and beat until light and creamy; pile on a hot dish; do not smooth the mound, but leave it irregular; serve immediately.

RICED POTATOES.

Prepare the potatoes as for mashed potato; press through a potato-ricer into a hot dish; put the dish in the oven for five minutes.

BAKED POTATOES.

Select potatoes of uniform size; scrub and remove any imperfections in the skin; wipe dry and put into a hot oven; bake about forty-five minutes, or until the potato is soft, when pressed between the fingers; when baked cut a slit lengthwise in the potato and press the potato gently; remove immediately from the oven; cover with a towel until serving time; send baked potatoes to the table covered with a doily to protect them from the cold air.

BAKED POTATOES WITH ROAST BEEF

Pare small potatoes and put into the pan with the roast beef about half an hour before the meat is cooked; arrange on the dish with the beef.

FRENCH FRIED POTATOES.

Pare and cut into six pieces on the length of the potato; let stand in cold water two or three hours; wipe, and fry in very hot fat; drain; dust with salt and serve with steak or chops.

POTATO BALLS.

Pare eight or ten large potatoes; with a vegetable scoop cut little balls from the potato; drop them into ice water and let stand two or three hours; wipe and put in the frying basket; lower gently into very hot fat; cook until nicely browned—about five minutes; drain; dredge with salt and serve very hot.

CREAMED POTATOES.

One quart of cold boiled potatoes cut in half-inch dice; one pint of white sauce; one tablespoonful of minced parsley; pepper and salt; season the potatoes with pepper and salt; add to the white sauce and cook slowly until the potatoes are hot; add the parsley and stir carefully; serve immediately.

LYONNAISE POTATOES.

One quart of cold boiled potatoes, cut into dice,
Three tablespoonfuls of clarified butter,
Two tablespoonfuls minced onion,
One tablespoonful minced parsley,
Salt and pepper.

Season the potatoes with salt and pepper; brown the onion lightly in the clarified butter; add the potatoes and the parsley, cooking until nicely browned, being careful not to break them; serve immediately on a hot dish.

SWEET POTATOES.

Wash and cover with boiling salted water; boil gently until tender, or parboil the potatoes; pare and cut in halves; dust lightly with sugar, salt and pepper; put two tablespoonfuls of clarified butter into a small dripping pan; lay the potatoes on the pan and bake in a hot oven.

BOILED RICE.

Pick over and wash one cupful of rice; drop gradually into two quarts of rapidly boiling salted water, and boil rapidly until the rice is soft; drain in a sieve; hold the sieve under the faucet and let the cold water run through it; shake well; turn out on a shallow pan and set in a moderate oven to dry; stir occasionally.

BOILED MACARONI.

Two quarts of boiling water; two teaspoonfuls of salt; six sticks of macaroni; break the macaroni into inch pieces; wash and drop into the salted water; boil rapidly for thirty minutes; drain; hold colander under faucet and let the cold water run over the macaroni; shake well and drain.

MACARONI AND CREAM SAUCE.

Make a white sauce; season the boiled macaroni with pepper and salt; mix with the white sauce and simmer for five minutes.

MACARONI AND TOMATO SAUCE.

Cook the macaroni as directed; add to one pint of tomato sauce. and simmer five minutes.

MACARONI AND CHEESE.

One pint of white sauce,	One cupful of grated cheese,
Six sticks of macaroni,	One-half cupful of bread crumbs,
One tablespoonful of butter,	Pepper and salt.

Boil the macaroni; butter the baking dish; put a layer of macaroni in the bottom; sprinkle thickly with cheese; pour over it a cupful of white sauce, then another layer of macaroni, more cheese and white sauce; moisten the crumbs with the butter, melted; spread on top and bake in a moderate oven until the crumbs are brown.

BOILED ONIONS.

Peel; cover with boiling salted water; cook slowly for ten minutes; drain off the water and add more; cook for half an hour, or until tender; drain and cover with milk and simmer gently for ten minutes; season with pepper, salt and butter, and serve.

TOMATOES.

Scald; peel and set on ice about two hours before serving; slice and serve with sugar, salt and vinegar or mayonnaise dressing.

ESCALLOPED TOMATOES.

One quart can of tomatoes,	One saltspoonful of pepper,
One teaspoonful of salt,	Two tablespoonfuls of sugar,
Four slices of stale bread,	One cupful of bread crumbs.
One tablespoonful of butter,	

Butter the baking dish; cut the bread into small squares; season the tomatoes with pepper and salt; put a layer of bread in the bottom of baking dish; pour over it some of the tomatoes, another layer of bread and more tomatoes, until the material is used; moisten the bread crumbs with melted butter; spread over the top; bake in moderate oven twenty minutes, or until the crumbs are nicely browned.

CAULIFLOWER.

Pick off the outside leaves; soak in cold water for about an hour; cook in boiling salted water until tender; drain; cover with cream sauce, and serve.

CABBAGE.

Remove the outside leaves; cut into quarters and remove the tough portion; cook in boiling salted water; drain; chop fine; season with pepper, salt and butter.

SPINACH. .

Pick over and wash thoroughly; put into a kettle with just enough water to keep it from burning; boil until tender; drain and chop fine; season with pepper, salt and butter; garnish with hard-boiled eggs.

ASPARAGUS.

Wash carefully; tie into bundles; cover with boiling, slightly salted water, and boil for fifteen minutes, or until the asparagus is tender; drain; season with pepper, salt and butter, or pour a white sauce over it and serve on toast.   Asparagus may be served cold with a mayonnaise dressing.   The water in which the asparagus is boiled can be used for soup.

BEANS.

Remove the strings; cut into inch pieces; wash and cook in boiling salted water for two or three hours, or until the beans are tender; drain; season with butter, pepper and salt; when very young they will cook in much shorter time.

GREEN PEAS.

Wash the pods before shelling; cover the pods with boiling, slightly salted water; cook ten minutes; skim out the pods and put in the peas; boil until tender; the fresh pods are sweet and very highly flavored; let the water boil nearly away; season with butter, pepper and salt; a little sugar and sweet cream may be added.

SWEET CORN.

Remove the husk and silk; put into boiling water; cover and cook from five to fifteen minutes; take up the corn as soon as the raw taste is destroyed.

⁘ Bread ⁘

VIENNA BREAD.

Flour,   One compressed yeast cake,
One pint of wetting (half milk   One teaspoonful of salt.
    and water),

Dissolve the yeast in half a cupful of cold water; add the salt to the wetting, which should be luke warm, or at a temperature of about eighty degrees, then add the yeast; stir in flour enough to make a stiff batter; beat thoroughly; add enough more flour to make a soft dough; turn out on a well-floured bread board and knead until soft and velvety; when it will not stick to the hands or board there is sufficient flour; put into a buttered bowl; brush the top with melted butter or drippings; cover with a towel and let rise for three hours, or until it is double its bulk; the dough should be kept at a temperature of seventy-five degrees; when the dough is light, shape into loaves or rolls and put on the pans; butter the top and allow it to stand one hour, or until it is light; bake in a hot oven; the oven for baking bread should be hot enough to brown a small quantity of flour in two minutes; bake until nicely browned all over; it requires from forty-five minutes to one hour to bake a loaf of bread.

FRENCH ROLLS.

Take a small piece of dough about four inches square; shape into a ball; roll under the palms of the hands upon the bread board into a long roll about one inch in diameter; lay in a buttered roll pan; butter the top lightly; cover with a towel and let rise one hour, or until double its bulk; bake in a hot oven twenty minutes, or until nicely browned; · cool the bread and rolls where a draught of fresh air will pass around the bread.

SOUP STICKS.

Take a small bit of Vienna dough about one inch and a half square; roll into a long stick; lay in buttered soup-stick pans, or about half an inch apart on a flat pan; butter the top lightly; bake immediately in a hot oven until nicely browned; serve with soup.

MILK BREAD.

| One quart of milk, | Two teaspoonfuls of salt, |
| One compressed yeast cake, | Flour enough to make a soft dough. |

Dissolve the yeast in one-half cupful of cold water; heat the milk to about eighty degrees; add the salt and dissolve yeast; mix in flour enough to make a soft dough; beat well; turn out on bread board and knead until soft and velvety; put into a buttered bowl; brush the top with melted fat; cover and let rise for five hours, or until double its bulk; shape into loaves; butter the top and let rise one hour; bake.

PARKER HOUSE ROLLS.

Take a piece of lightened milk-bread dough; roll into a sheet about one-half inch in thickness; let the dough shrink; cut the rolls with a large cutter; pull into an oval shape; spread with softened butter and fold over, having the edges come together; brush the top with butter and let rise one hour, or until light; bake.

TWIN ROLLS.

Cut the rolls from a sheet of dough a quarter of an inch in thickness; put two rolls together, spreading softened butter between; let rise for one hour and bake.

GRAHAM BREAD.

One pint milk and water (equal parts),
One compressed yeast cake,
One tablespoonful of sugar,
One teaspoonful of salt.

Dissolve the yeast in one-half cupful of cold water; have the wetting luke warm and add to it the yeast, sugar and salt; mix in enough graham flour, sifted, to make a soft dough; flour the board well with white flour; turn out the dough and knead until it ceases to stick to the board; let rise for three hours, then shape into loaves; let rise one hour, or until it is light; then bake.

BOSTON BROWN BREAD.

Two cupfuls of cornmeal,
Two cupfuls of graham flour,
One cupful of molasses,
One teaspoonful of salt,
Two teaspoonfuls of soda,
Three cupfuls of buttermilk.

Mix the cornmeal, graham flour, salt and soda together; add the molasses and the buttermilk gradually; fill mould two-thirds full; steam in single mould six hours—in small moulds two or three hours.

GERMAN COFFEE CAKE.

One and one-half yeast cakes,
Three eggs,
Three tablespoonfuls of sugar,
One teaspoonful of salt,
One pint of milk,
Three tablespoonfuls of butter.

Cover the yeast with cold water; beat the eggs until light; heat the milk scalding hot; pour the hot milk over the beaten egg; add the sugar and salt and allow it to stand until cool (about 80 degrees); add the yeast, and flour enough to make a soft dough; turn out on a well-floured bread board and knead until smooth; put into a buttered bowl; cover and let rise three hours, or until light; soften the butter and mix it thoroughly into the dough; allow it to rise again for two hours; roll into a sheet one inch in thickness and put into a buttered pan; spread with melted butter; dredge with sugar and cinnamon and let rise one hour; bake in a moderate oven thirty-five minutes.

BUNS.

Take a piece of coffee-cake dough; shape into round buns; place half an inch apart on a buttered pan; brush the top with melted butter; let rise one hour and bake in a moderate oven.

CINNAMON ROLLS.

Roll a piece of coffee-cake dough in a sheet one-fourth inch in thickness; cut into strips; brush with melted butter; dust with sugar and cinnamon; roll into shape; place one inch apart on a buttered pan and let rise one hour; bake in a moderately hot oven.

JENNY LIND.

Take a large piece of coffee-cake dough and mix with it half a cupful of currants or stoned raisins; roll into a sheet half an inch in thickness; cut in circular shape; brush the top with melted butter; fold over, leaving the top edge one inch from the under edge; raise one hour; bake in a moderate oven from thirty to forty-five minutes.

BAKING POWDER BISCUIT.

One quart of flour,	Two tablespoonfuls of butter,
Two teaspoonfuls of baking powder,	Sweet milk enough to make a soft dough.
One teaspoonful of salt,	

Sift the flour before it is measured; sift flour, salt and baking powder together; rub the butter into it with the fingers; add the milk and beat to a smooth dough; turn out upon the bread board; dust with flour and roll into a sheet three-quarters of an inch thick; cut into small biscuit; butter the biscuit pan and dust lightly with flour; lay the biscuit close together and bake in a hot oven ten minutes.

QUICK SWEDISH ROLLS.

Roll a piece of baking-powder biscuit dough into a sheet one half inch in thickness; spread with softened butter; dust with cinnamon and sugar; roll like a jelly roll; with a sharp knife cut off bits from the end about one-half inch; lay the flat side on a well-buttered pan; bake in a hot oven ten minutes. These make a very good substitute for cinnamon rolls; to be served hot.

SHORTCAKE.

One pint of flour,	One egg,
One-half teaspoonful of salt,	Two tablespoonfuls of butter,
One and one-half teaspoonfuls of baking powder,	One-half cupful of milk.

Sift the flour, salt and baking powder together; rub the butter into the flour; beat the egg until light; add the milk; beat, do not knead, the dough; turn out on a well-floured board; roll into sheets one-half inch in thickness; butter and flour the baking pan; lay a sheet of the cake in the pan; brush the top with melted butter; put on a second sheet; bake in a moderate oven fifteen or twenty minutes; when baked separate the sheets; put a layer of fruit, sprinkled with powdered sugar, between, another layer of fruit on top and cover with whipped cream; strawberries, raspberries, pineapple, oranges, or any kind of fruit desired may be used.

MUFFINS.

Two cupfuls of flour,	Two tablespoonfuls of melted butter,
Two teaspoonfuls of baking powder,	Two eggs,
One cupful of milk,	One-half saltspoonful of salt.

Sift the flour, baking powder and salt together; separate the eggs; add the yolks and the milk gradually to the flour; beat to a smooth batter; add the melted butter; beat the whites of the eggs stiff and add last; bake in gem pans in a hot oven half an hour.

SALLY LUNNS.

Two cupfuls of flour,
One and one-half teaspoonfuls of baking powder,
One-half teaspoonful of salt,
One-half cupful of milk,
Two eggs,
Two tablespoonfuls of sugar,
One-third cupful of butter.

Sift the flour, salt, sugar and baking powder together; separate the eggs and beat separately; add the yolks and milk to the flour and beat thoroughly, then the melted butter and lastly the whites of the eggs beaten stiff; bake in gem pans in a hot oven for fifteen minutes.

RAISED MUFFINS.

One egg,
One cupful of milk,
Two cupfuls of flour,
One-half teaspoonful of salt,
Two tablespoonfuls of sugar,
One-half yeast cake,
One tablespoonful of melted butter.

Cover the yeast cake with cold water and let it dissolve; heat the milk scalding hot; beat the egg, salt and sugar together; pour the hot milk over the beaten egg; let stand until luke warm, then add the yeast and flour; beat to a smooth batter; let rise for four or five hours; fill muffin pans two-thirds full; let rise from twenty to thirty minutes; bake in a hot oven.

GRAHAM GEMS.

One and one-half cupfuls of graham flour, sifted,
One cupful of milk,
One tablespoonful of sugar,
One tablespoonful of melted butter,
One-half teaspoonful of salt,
One egg,
Two teaspoonfuls of baking powder.

Mix the flour, salt and baking powder together; beat the egg; add the sugar and beat together, then the milk; mix the flour into the egg and milk and beat to a smooth batter; add the melted butter; bake in buttered gem pans in a hot oven.

POPOVERS.

One cupful of flour,
One egg,
One-half teaspoonful of salt,
One cupful of milk.

Beat the egg very light; add the milk and beat together; mix the flour and salt; add half a cupful of the liquid and mix to a smooth batter; beat thoroughly, then add the rest of the milk and beat; heat buttered iron gem pans hissing hot; half fill with the mixture; bake in a hot oven thirty-five or forty minutes.

GRIDDLE CAKES.

One cupful of flour,	One-half teaspoonful of salt,
One cupful of buttermilk,	One-half teaspoonful of soda.
One egg,	

Mix the flour, salt and soda together; separate the egg; add the yolk to the flour and gradually add the buttermilk; beat the white of the egg stiff; add to the batter; if sour milk is used instead of buttermilk add one tablespoonful of melted butter; have the griddle hot; grease it with a piece of fat pork.

FLANNEL CAKES.

Two cupfuls of flour,	Two eggs,
Cup and a half of milk,	One-half teaspoonful of salt,
One tablespoonful of melted butter,	Two teaspoonfuls of baking powder.

Sift the flour, baking powder and salt together; separate the eggs; add the yolks unbeaten to the flour and the milk gradually; beat to a smooth batter; beat the whites of the eggs stiff; add the melted butter to the batter, and lastly the beaten whites of the eggs; cook on a hot griddle.

WAFFLES.

Two cupfuls of flour,	Cup and one-fourth of milk,
Two teaspoonfuls of baking powder,	Three eggs,
One teaspoonful of salt,	One tablespoonful of melted butter.

Mix the flour, salt and baking powder together; separate the eggs and add the yolks to the flour; add the milk gradually and beat to a smooth batter; add the melted butter and lastly the whites of the eggs, beaten stiff; heat the waffle iron hissing hot; butter with clarified butter; fill the waffle iron two-thirds full; close the iron and cook one minute, then turn and cook two or three minutes on the other side; serve with maple syrup or caramel syrup.

CARAMEL SYRUP.

Cook one cupful of sugar and one-fourth cupful of water over a hot fire, without stirring until it begins to brown; then stir until of a rich golden brown; add one-half cupful of water and stir over the fire until smooth; serve with waffles.

❯⟩ Eggs ⟨❮

SOFT BOILED EGGS.

Put two eggs in a saucepan; cover with boiling water; cover and let stand eight minutes. This method will cook both white and yolk. If you are cooking a large number of eggs cover with boiling water and let stand five minutes; pour off and add more boiling water; let stand five minutes longer.

HARD BOILED EGGS.

Cover the eggs with boiling water and boil twenty minutes. Cooking eggs ten minutes makes the yolks leatherly and indigestible; cooking twenty minutes makes them light and mealy.

SHIRRED EGGS.

Butter a sauce plate; separate two eggs, taking care not to break the yolks; beat the whites stiff; pile up irregularly upon the sauce plate; make two nests in the whites; slip in the yolks; bake in cool oven until the white is lightly browned; season with pepper, salt and a bit of butter, and serve.

SHIRRED EGGS, NO. 2.

Butter individual plates; break carefully two eggs into each; season with pepper, salt and bits of butter; bake in a moderate oven until the white is set.

POACHED EGGS.

To one quart of water add one tablespoonful of salt and boil slowly; break the eggs carefully and slip into the water; dip the water over the eggs; loosen carefully from the bottom of the pan; when the white is set lift on a skimmer; trim the edges and slip onto toast.

SCRAMBLED EGGS.

Four eggs,	One-half teaspoonful of salt.
One tablespoonful of butter,	

Break the eggs with a fork; add the salt; melt the butter in omelet pan; pour in the beaten eggs; stir for two minutes over a hot fire, and serve.

FRENCH OMELET.

Five eggs,	Five tablespoonfuls of water,
One tablespoonful of clarified butter,	Pepper and salt.

Break the eggs with a fork; add the water and beat together; have omelet pan perfectly smooth; put the clarified butter in the pan; when it begins to sizzle pour in the omelet and shake vigorously over the fire until the omelet thickens on the bottom; with a fork lift the cooked egg and let the uncooked run under; season with pepper and salt; loosen from the sides of the pan with a flexible knife and slip the knife under the omelet; fold and turn onto a hot dish; serve immediately. Grated cheese, chopped ham, chicken or parsley can be sprinkled on before folding the omelet.

LIGHT OMELET.

Four eggs,	Half a teaspoonful of salt,
Four tablespoonfuls of milk,	One teaspoonful of clarified butter.

Separate the eggs; beat the yolks and milk together; add the salt; beat the whites stiff and add to the mixture; melt the butter in an omelet pan; turn in the egg mixture and cook until nicely browned underneath; set in a cool oven until the egg is firm; loosen from the pan; fold and serve immediately.

⚬ Pastry and Pies ⚬

FLAKY PASTRY.

One cupful of flour,	One-third cupful of shortening,
One saltspoonful of salt,	One-fourth cupful of ice water.

Have all the material cold; put the flour and salt into a chopping bowl; add the shortening (half butter and half lard) and chop into pieces the size of a pea; moisten the pastry with the ice water, mixing lightly with a fork; turn out on a floured board; draw together into oblong shape; roll back and forth into an oblong sheet; fold into thirds; turn half way around and roll back and forth; fold again and turn half way around and roll out for a third time; brush off all the surplus flour; roll like a jelly roll; wrap in a napkin and set on ice; it can be used immediately, or stand on ice until the next day.

PUFF PASTE.

One cupful of ice water,	One teaspoonful of salt,
One pound of flour,	White of one egg.
One pound of butter,	

Have material and utensils cold; wash the butter in cold water and knead with a spoon until it becomes waxy; shape into an oblong sheet about an inch in thickness and set it in a pan of ice water; mix the salt and flour together; rub one-third of the butter into the flour; moisten with the egg and ice water; mix with a knife; stir vigorously; dredge the board lightly with flour; turn out the paste; sprinkle lightly with flour; roll backward and forward; turn the paste half way around and roll from you; when about one-fourth of an inch in thickness wipe the remainder of the butter and lay it on the paste; sprinkle lightly with flour; fold the paste from each side until the edges meet, then fold from the ends; pound lightly and roll back and forth two or three times; double the paste and roll down to one-half inch in thickness; fold in thirds and turn half way around; roll down again; repeat this for six times; place on ice to harden for one or two hours before using; if the paste sticks place it on ice; when chilled it will roll more easily; use as little flour as possible.

MINCE PIE.

Lean beef, four pounds,	Four pounds of currants,
Two pounds of suet,	Half a pound of citron,
Four quarts of chopped apples,	Juice of six lemons,
Five pounds of sugar,	One pint of molasses,
Four pounds of raisins,	Three quinces,
Three quarts of sweet cider,	One pint of brandy,
Cloves, cinnamon, mace, and nutmeg — three tablespoonfuls of each,	Three ounces each of candied orange and lemon peel,
	One pint of white wine,
Two cupfuls of meat broth,	Two tablespoonfuls of salt.

Cook and mince the meat fine; chop the suet fine; cook the quinces in the cider until soft; chop the citron, lemon and orange peel; mix all the ingredients and cook slowly until the apples are soft; add the brandy and wine last; pack away in jars covered tightly; take half the flaky pastry; roll into a sheet one-fourth inch in thickness; cover the piepan, putting the pastry on quite full; fill with mince meat, having it about half an inch thick; roll out the other half of the pastry about one-eighth inch in thickness; fold over and cut two or three slits; cover the pie and bake in a moderate oven.

LEMON PIE.

Grated rind of one lemon,	Three-quarters of a cupful of boiling water,
Two level tablespoonfuls of corn starch.	of two eggs,
Three-quarters of a cupful of sugar,	teaspoonful of butter,
	Juice of one lemon.

Mix the cornstarch and sugar together and add to the boiling water, stirring until it thickens; add the grated rind of the lemon and cook for ten minutes; beat the yolks of the eggs until creamy; add slowly to the cornstarch; cooking two minutes longer; remove from the fire and add the lemon juice and butter; line a piepan with flaky pastry and a rim; cover with wax paper; fill with pieces of stale bread and bake in a moderate oven; when baked remove the paper and fill with the mixture; beat the whites of the eggs stiff; add two tablespoonfuls of sugar and beat together; cover the pie with the meringue and bake in a cool oven until lightly browned.

JUICY FRUIT PIES.

Line a piepan with pastry; fill with ..n old piece of linen; put on the upper crust and bake in a moderate oven; stew the fruit; season to taste; when the pastry is baked separate with a sharp knife; remove the linen; fill with fruit; place the cover on top and set aside to cool; many of these shells can be baked at one time and filled when required, but the pastry must be reheated; remember to put the filling into the pie while both are hot.

CUSTARD PIE.

Line a piepan with pastry and a rim; dust lightly with flour; scald three cupfuls of milk; beat three eggs until creamy; add three table-spoonfuls of sugar and beat together; pour the scalded milk over the beaten egg; add one saltspoonful of salt and one saltspoonful of nut-meg; fill the piepan and bake slowly; as soon as it puffs up test with a knife; if it comes out clean it is done.

❖ Puddings ❖

ENGLISH PLUM PUDDING.

One-half pound of stale bread crumbs,
One cupful of hot milk,
One-half cupful of sugar,
Four eggs,
One-half pound of raisins,
One-half pound of currants,
One-fourth pound of figs,
One-eighth pound of citron,
One-half pound of suet,
One-fourth cup of brandy,
One-half teaspoonful each of cinna-
mon, mace, cloves, nutmeg,
One teaspoonful of salt.

Cover the bread crumbs with the milk; separate the eggs; beat the yolks until creamy; add the sugar and beat together; add to the bread and milk; chop and flour the figs and suet; add all the ingredients to the bread and milk; beat whites of the eggs stiff and add to the mixture; butter the mould; fill three-quarters full; steam in a single mould from five to twelve hours; serve with brandy sauce.

STEAMED SUET PUDDING.

Three cupfuls of flour,
One level teaspoonful of soda,
One cup of chopped suet,
One cup of raisins and currants,
One cup of water,
One cup of molasses,
One teaspoonful each of cinnamon,
nutmeg and cloves.

Mix the flour, soda, spices and suet together; add the molasses, fruit and water; steam three hours in a single mould, or one hour in small moulds; serve hot, with fruit sauce.

ORANGE PUDDING.

One cupful of bread crumbs,   Yolks of two eggs,
Juice and rind of one-half orange,   Whites of four eggs.
One-third cup of sugar,

Cover the bread crumbs with milk; add the rind and juice of the orange and the beaten yolks of the eggs; beat the whites until stiff; add the sugar and beat and add to the mixture; bake in a buttered mould; set in a pan of hot water; bake until firm; serve with golden sauce.

FRENCH BREAD PUDDING.

One cupful of bread crumbs,   One saltspoonful of salt,
Two cupfuls of milk,   One tablespoonful of sugar,
Two small eggs,   .   One teaspoonful of butter.

Scald the milk and pour it over the bread crumbs; separate the eggs and beat the yolks with the sugar; add to the bread crumbs; add salt and the butter, melted; pour into a buttered baking dish; set in a pan of hot water; bake in a moderate oven until firm; when cooked spread with jelly; beat the whites of the eggs stiff; add two tablespoonfuls of powdered sugar and beat together; cover the pudding with the meringue and bake in a cool oven until nicely browned.

PRUNE PUDDING.

One-half pound of prunes,   One-quarter teaspoonful of salt,
One pint of water,   Juice of one-half lemon,
One cupful of sugar,   Six level tablespoonfuls of cornstarch.

Wash the prunes and soak over night; simmer until tender; remove the pits; add enough water to the liquid to make two cupfuls; mix the cornstarch with the sugar; add to the prunes and cook fifteen minutes, stirring frequently; when cooked add the lemon juice and one-half teaspoonful of almond extract; dip the mould in cold water and drain; fill with the pudding and set away to cool; serve cold with whipped cream.

DELICATE PUDDING.

Four level tablespoonfuls of corn- One and one-half cupfuls of boiling
   starch.   water,
One-fourth cupful of cold water,   One-half cupful of sugar,
Whites of three eggs,   One teaspoonful of vanilla.

Mix the cornstarch with the cold water; pour over it the boiling water and cook fifteen minutes; beat the eggs stiff; add the sugar and beat together; pour the hot starch over the egg and sugar and stir until smooth; add the vanilla; dip mould in water; fill with pudding; set on ice; serve with boiled custard made from the yolks of the eggs.

BOILED CUSTARD.

One pint of milk,	Three tablespoonfuls of sugar,
Yolks of three eggs,	One-half teaspoonful of vanilla.

Scald the milk; beat the eggs and sugar together; pour the hot milk over the beaten egg; cook until creamy; add the vanilla and set aside to cool.

CREAM RICE PUDDING.

One-fourth cup of rice,	One tablespoonful of sugar,
Two and one-quarter cupfuls of milk,	Saltspoonful of salt.

Wash the rice; add the milk, sugar and salt and allow it to come to the boiling point; simmer slowly and cook for two or three hours, stirring occasionally; when the rice is tender put on the grate in a hot oven and brown; serve hot or cold.

BREAD AND APPLE PUDDING.

Four tart apples,	Salt, sugar and cinnamon.
Two slices of stale bread,	

Butter the baking dish; pare, core and slice the apples; soak the bread in cold water; put a layer of apples in the bottom of the baking dish; sprinkle with sugar and cinnamon and a little salt; put a layer of bread, another layer of apples and cover the top with stale bread crumbs; moisten with melted butter; bake in a moderate oven for half an hour; cover the first fifteen minutes; serve hot with lemon sauce.

STRAWBERRY ROLY-POLY.

Two cupfuls of flour,	Half a teaspoonful of salt,
Two teaspoonfuls of baking powder,	One-third cupful of butter,
	Two eggs,
One-fourth cupful of sugar,	Two-thirds of a cupful of milk.

Sift the flour, salt, baking powder and sugar together; rub in the butter; beat the eggs until creamy; add the milk to the eggs and beat together; mix thoroughly; turn out on a well-floured board and roll into a sheet half an inch in thickness; spread with the strawberries and dust with equal parts of sugar and flour; roll like a jelly roll; wrap in a napkin and steam from an hour to an hour and a half; serve hot with strawberry sauce.

PRUNE SOUFFLÉ.

One-half pound of prunes,	Whites of six eggs,
One-half teaspoonful of salt,	Six tablespoonfuls of sugar.
Juice of one lemon,	

Wash and soak the prunes over night; stew until very soft; remove the pits and chop very fine; add the lemon juice; beat the whites of the eggs very stiff; add the sugar and salt and beat together; beat in the chopped prunes; put in buttered baking dish and bake in a cool oven thirty minutes; serve immediately, with creamy sauce.

BAKED CORNMEAL PUDDING.

Scald one pint of milk; moisten one and one-half tablespoonfuls of cornmeal with a little cold milk; pour over it the hot milk and cook in a double boiler for two hours, stirring frequently; then add one level tablespoonful of butter, one-half teaspoonful of salt, two tablespoonfuls of molasses, two eggs and one pint of cold milk; butter a baking dish and fill with the mixture; bake in a moderate oven one hour; set the baking dish into a pan of hot water.

❀ Pudding Sauces ❀

GOLDEN SAUCE.

One-third cupful of butter,	One-third cupful of milk,
One cupful of sugar (powdered),	Grated rind of half an orange.
Yolks of two eggs,	

Cream the butter; add the sugar and cream together; then add the yolks of the eggs and orange rind; heat the milk scalding hot; pour onto the butter; cook until it thickens.

LEMON SAUCE.

One cupful of water,	One-half cupful of sugar,
Rind of half a lemon,	One teaspoonful of cornstarch,
One teaspoonful of butter,	Juice of one large lemon.

Mix cornstarch with sugar; cook sugar, water, cornstarch and rind of the lemon together for ten minutes; remove from the fire and add butter and lemon juice.

WINE SAUCE.

Cream one cupful of butter; add two cupfuls of powdered sugar and cream together; heat a cupful of wine and add slowly; cook over boiling water for two minutes.

CARAMEL SAUCE.

Cook together one cupful of sugar and one-fourth of a cupful of water; boil rapidly until it begins to brown; then stir until of a rich golden brown; add one-half cupful of water and stir until smooth.

BRANDY SAUCE.

Cook one cupful of sugar and half a cupful of water for fifteen minutes; beat the yolks of three eggs and stir them into the boiling syrup; set the bowl into a pan of hot water and beat until it begins to thicken; add one tablespoonful of butter and the whites of three eggs beaten stiff; lastly add one-third of a cupful of brandy; stir thoroughly, and serve.

HARD SAUCE.

Beat half a cupful of butter to a cream; gradually add one cupful of powdered sugar and beat until creamy; flavor with one teaspoonful of any flavoring desired; beat the white of one egg stiff; add to the sugar and butter.

FOAMY SAUCE.

Beat butter and sugar together as for hard sauce; add one-third of a cupful of boiling milk, gradually beating all the time; serve immediately.

FRUIT SAUCE.

Cook one cupful of sugar, one tablespoonful of flour and one cupful of water together, for five minutes; add half a cupful of any kind of fruit juice; pour over one-half cupful of butter beaten to a cream.

CARAMEL CUSTARDS.

Three eggs.
One pint of milk,

Two-thirds cupful of caramelized sugar.

Scald the milk; beat the eggs; pour the hot milk over the beaten egg; add the sugar; pour into buttered custard cups; set the cups in pan of hot water; bake until firm; serve with caramel sauce.

❋ Invalid Cookery ❋

BEEF TEA.

Buy the top of the round for beef tea; it contains the most nutriment and is the best flavored; remove every particle of fat; cut the meat into very fine pieces; add one pint of water to each pound of beef; put into a glass jar and set the jar in a pan of warm water; do not heat the water above 110 degrees; let stand for two hours; strain through a strainer cloth; season with salt, and serve.

BROILED BEEF TEA.

Broil a thick round steak for five minutes; cut into small pieces and press out the juice; salt and serve, or if too strong add half a cupful of hot water.

OATMEAL GRUEL.

Cover three tablespoonfuls of oatmeal with one quart of boiling water; add one-fourth of a teaspoonful of salt; boil one hour; put into an oatmeal boiler and cook two hours; strain, and serve with cream and sugar.

TOAST.

Cut stale bread one-third of an inch in thickness; remove the crusts; place on the toaster on the back part of the stove, turning frequently until it is dry; push to the hottest parts of the stove and brown nicely; toast should be dry and crisp, not hard or soggy in the middle.

TARVENCE CHICKEN CUSTARD.

Scald together one cupful of chicken stock and one cupful of cream; add slowly one and a half tablespoonfuls of Tarvence, and stir until smooth; beat the yolks of two eggs until creamy; pour the hot Tarvence mixture over the beaten egg; return to the fire and cook until thickened; season with pepper, salt and a little celery salt; may be served hot or cold.

EGGNOG.

Beat the yolk of one egg until creamy; add one tablespoonful of sugar, one tablespoonful of wine or brandy and half a cupful of milk; add the white of the egg, beaten to a stiff froth, and lastly a little nutmeg.

❋ Cake ❋

NOTES ON CAKE MAKING.

Have the bowl warm, the butter soft, sugar fine; use a wooden spoon for beating; never mix cake in tin; have pans perfectly clean; do not grease the pans; paper the bottom of the pan, and, for butter cakes, butter lightly the upper side of the paper. When baked slip a knife around the edges of the cake to loosen it; let stand in the pan until you can handle the pan without a holder; let butterless cakes stand in the pan until cold; when a cake is nearly baked it will shrink from the sides of the pan.

ANGEL CAKE.

One cupful of egg white,	One cupful of sugar,
One-half a level teaspoonful of cream of tartar.	One cupful of flour,
	One teaspoonful of almond extract.

To the eggs add a pinch of salt; beat for one minute; sift in the cream of tartar and beat until stiff; sift the sugar and beat into the eggs; add the flavoring; sift the flour five times before measuring it; fold it into the cake quickly and lightly; paper the pan; *do not* butter it; pour the mixture into the pan; cover and put into a cool oven; after half an hour remove the cover; bake an hour; when baked turn the pan bottom side up; if the pan has not feet, set something under the sides, so a current of air can pass under and over it; let stand until cold.

SUNSHINE CAKE.

Make the same as Angel Cake, adding the yolks of five eggs, beaten light.

SPONGE CAKE.

Five eggs,
One cupful of sugar,
One cupful of pastry flour,
Rind and juice of half a lemon.

Separate the eggs; beat the whites until stiff; add the lemon juice; beat the yolks with a Dover egg-beater until creamy; add the sugar and grated rind of the lemon and beat together; add the whites, and lastly sift in the flour; line the cake pan with paper and bake in a cool oven one hour; when done it will shrink from the sides of the pan; turn upside down and let stand in the pan until cold.

DELICATE CAKE.

Three-fourths cupful of butter,
One and one-half cupfuls of sugar,
Two-thirds cupful of cold water,
One teaspoonful of lemon juice or one-fourth teaspoonful of cream tartar,
Two-thirds cupful of egg white,
Three cupfuls of flour and three slightly rounding teaspoonfuls of baking powder,
One teaspoonful of almond and mace extract (one-fourth mace).

Cream the butter; add the sugar gradually and cream together; add the eggs unbeaten, one-half at a time, and beat together until light; add lemon juice; sift the flour before measuring; add water and flour alternately; mix the baking powder with the last half cupful of the flour and sift into the cake; beat thoroughly, and add the flavoring; beat the cake for five minutes after everything is added; bake in a moderate oven—one loaf, fifty minutes.

LADY'S CAKE.

One cupful of butter,
One cupful of sugar,
Whites of eight eggs,
One teaspoonful of lemon juice,
Two cupfuls of flour,
One teaspoonful of baking powder,
One teaspoonful of almond extract.

Cream the butter; add half a cupful of the sugar gradually and cream together; to the whites of the eggs add a pinch of salt; beat with a wire egg-beater until stiff; beat in the lemon juice and add the other half cupful of sugar and beat together; add to the creamed butter and sugar; sift and measure the flour; mix the baking powder with the last half cup; sift into the batter; beat the cake thoroughly after everything is added; bake in a moderate oven fifteen minutes.

LEMON QUEENS.

One-half cupful of butter,
One cupful of sugar,
Rind of half a lemon,
One tablespoonful of lemon juice,
Four eggs,
One-fourth teaspoonful of salt,
One-fourth teaspoonful of soda,
One and one-fourth cupfuls of flour.

Cream the butter; add the sugar gradually and cream together; add the rind and juice of the lemon; add eggs, unbeaten, one at a time, and beat until smooth and light; mix the soda and salt with the flour and sift into the batter; bake in muffin pans thirty minutes in a moderate oven.

PLAIN LOAF CAKE.

Two-thirds of a cupful of butter,
One and one-third cupfuls of sugar,
Three and one-fourth cupfuls of baking powder,
Four eggs,
Three teaspoonfuls of baking powder,
One cupful of milk,
One teaspoonful of orange and vanilla extract (half and half).

Cream the butter; add the sugar gradually and cream together; add the eggs, unbeaten, two at a time, and beat until perfectly smooth; add the milk and flour alternately, mixing the baking powder with the last half cupful of the flour and sift into the cake; add the flavoring; bake in a moderate oven from forty to fifty minutes.

SPICE CAKE.

Two cupfuls of brown sugar,
Two cupfuls of flour,
One-half cupful of butter,
Four eggs,
One-half cupful of sour milk,
One level teaspoonful of soda,
One teaspoonful each of nutmeg, cinnamon and cloves.

Cream the butter; add the sugar gradually and cream together; add the yolks of four and the whites of two eggs; add the milk and flour alternately, mixing the spices and baking powder with the last half cupful of the flour; bake from thirty to forty-five minutes; ice with boiled icing.

COCOANUT CAKE.

One-third cupful of butter,
One cupful of sugar,
One-half cupful of milk,
Two eggs,
One and one-half cupfuls of flour,
One and one-half teaspoonfuls of baking powder.

Cream the butter; add the sugar gradually and cream together; add the eggs, unbeaten, and beat thoroughly; sift the flour and baking powder together; add the milk and flour alternately; bake in layers fifteen minutes in moderate oven.

COCOANUT ICING.

Beat the whites of two eggs stiff; add two cupfuls of powdered sugar and beat together; mix cocoanut with one-half the icing and spread between the layers; spread over the top and sides of the cake and sprinkle thickly with cocoanut on top and sides.

CHOCOLATE CAKE.

One-half cupful of butter,	Two and one-third cupfuls of flour,
One cupful of sugar,	Two teaspoonfuls of baking powder,
Whites of five eggs,	One teaspoonful of vanilla and
One teaspoonful of lemon juice,	lemon (half of each).
One-half cupful of milk,	

Cream the butter; add the sugar gradually and cream together; add the whites of the eggs and lemon juice and beat thoroughly, then the flour and milk alternately; sift the baking powder with the last half cupful of flour; bake in two thick layers in a moderate oven twenty minutes; make an icing of one-third cupful of egg white, one and one-half cupfuls of confectioners' sugar, two ounces of unsweetened chocolate, one teaspoonful of vanilla; beat the sugar and whites of the eggs together for five minutes; cut the chocolate into small pieces and set in a bowl over the teakettle; add the melted chocolate to the sugar and beat until it will pile up in the bowl when dropped from the egg-beater; put a thick filling between the layers and spread over the top and sides; let stand until it hardens.

POUND CAKE.

One cupful of butter,	One cupful of sugar,
Five eggs,	Two cupfuls of pastry flour,
One teaspoonful of baking pow-der,	One teaspoonful of extract—vanilla, lemon and a few drops of mace.

Cream the butter and gradually add the sugar and cream together; add the eggs, unbeaten, one at a time, beating at least three minutes between each egg; add the flour sifted, mixing the baking powder with the last half cupful of the flour; lastly add the extracts, beating the cake thoroughly; bake in a loaf in moderate oven fifty minutes; if baked in a sheet it may be cut in fancy shapes and iced with confectioners' icing.

A white fruit cake is made by adding one cupful of stoned raisins or currants, or one quarter of a pound of citron, to the batter.

FRUIT CAKE.

One pound of butter,
One dozen eggs,
Five pounds of raisins,
One cupful of molasses,
One pint of brandy,
One-half pint of wine,
One pound of flour,

One pound of sugar,
One pound of citron,
Three pounds of currants.
One tablespoonful each of cinnamon, cloves, mace, allspice, and nutmeg,
Two level teaspoonfuls of soda.

Cream the butter; add the sugar gradually and cream together; beat the eggs until creamy and add to the butter and sugar, then add the molasses; sift the flour, soda and spices together and add gradually, beating thoroughly; stone and chop the raisins; chop the citron; add the fruit, wine and brandy and mix thoroughly; line a large pan with two thicknesses of heavy brown paper; butter lightly; bake in a moderate oven three hours.

GINGERBREAD.

Three cupfuls of flour,
One and one-half cupfuls of molasses,
One-half cupful of milk,

One-half cupful of lard or butter,
One egg,
One-half teaspoonful of soda,
One teaspoonful of ginger.

Sift the flour and ginger together; add the molasses, milk, beaten egg, butter or lard softened; dissolve the soda in the milk; bake in a moderate oven; care must be taken not to have the oven too hot; molasses cakes burn more readily than other cakes.

HOT WATER GINGERBREAD.

One cupful of molasses,
One teaspoonful of soda,
One-half teaspoonful of salt,
One-half cupful of boiling water,

One tablespoonful of ginger,
One tablespoonful of melted butter,
Two cupfuls of flour.

Mix the molasses, ginger, soda, salt, butter and boiling water together; add the flour, sifted; bake in a hot oven twenty minutes.

CREAM PUFFS.

One cupful of boiling water,
One-half cupful of butter,

One cupful of flour,
Four eggs.

Put the water and butter in saucepan and boil slowly until the butter is melted; then add the flour and allow it to cook until it cleans from the sides of the pan, stirring constantly; when cool, add one egg at a time, beating it in thoroughly; drop, by small spoonfuls, on a buttered papered pan; bake in a moderate oven until puffed and crusty—about thirty minutes; when cold, cut on one side and fill with whipped cream, sweetened with powdered sugar and flavored with vanilla or with a filling made from "filling for Cream Puffs."

FILLING FOR CREAM PUFFS.

Two cupfuls of milk,
Three-fourths of a cupful of sugar,
One teaspoonful of vanilla.

One-third of a cupful of flour,
Two eggs.

Scald the milk; mix the sugar and flour together and beat into the eggs; pour hot milk over the beaten egg; cook in a double boiler until thickened, stirring constantly; when cool flavor with vanilla.

FROSTING.

White of one egg.
One tablespoonful of lemon juice,

One cupful of confectioners' sugar.

Add the sugar gradually to the unbeaten white of the egg; when all the sugar is added beat in the lemon juice and one-half teaspoonful of vanilla; beat until it will pile up in the bowl when dropped from the egg-beater.

BOILED ICING.

One cupful of granulated sugar, One-fourth of a cupful of water.

Boil the water and sugar together until it will form a soft ball when dropped in ice water; beat the white of an egg until stiff; pour the boiling syrup over the beaten white of the egg and stir until it thickens; flavor with any desired flavoring.

CHOCOLATE ICING.

Two squares of unsweetened chocolate,
Three-fourths of a cupful of sugar,

One and one-half tablespoonfuls milk.
One egg.

Scrape the chocolate; add the milk and sugar; cook until it boils; beat the egg light and creamy; pour the chocolate mixture over the egg; cook one minute longer.

JELLY ROLL.

Four eggs,
Three-fourths of a cupful of pastry flour,

One-half of a cupful of powdered sugar.

Separate the eggs; beat the yolks until creamy; add the sugar and beat together; beat the whites until very stiff and dry and add to the yolks; sift into the flour and stir quickly; paper a large shallow pan; bake twenty minutes; while yet warm cut off the edges, spread with any kind of jelly and roll up; pin a towel around it and put in a cool place; cut with a sharp knife.

WAFERS.

One-half cupful of butter,
One-half cupful of milk.

Two cupfuls of flour,
One cupful of powdered sugar.

Cream the butter and gradually add the sugar and cream together: add the milk and flour alternately and mix thoroughly; spread on a sheet iron or turn baking pans bottom side up and wipe very clean; cut into squares when lightly browned and roll while hot; the wafers must be cut and rolled as soon as it comes from the oven.

COOKIES.

One cupful of butter.	Two cupfuls of sugar,
Three cupfuls of flour,	One egg,
One-half teaspoonful of soda,	One tablespoonful of milk.

Cream the butter and gradually add the sugar and cream together; beat the egg until light; dissolve the soda in the milk; add to the creamed butter and sugar; then add the flour: roll thin; cut into round cakes and bake quickly: seeds may be added, or any flavoring to taste.

CARAMEL FROSTING.

One cupful of brown sugar,	One ounce of chocolate.
One tablespoonful of water,	

Scrape the chocolate; add the sugar and water; cook gently twenty minutes.

❈ Delicate Desserts ❈

STRAWBERRY PUDDING.

One-third of a box of gelatine,	One and one-third cupfuls of straw-
One-third of a cupful of cold water,	berry juice,
	Juice of one lemon,
One-third of a cupful of boiling water,	Whites of two small eggs,
One saltspoonful of salt,	Six tablespoonfuls of whipped cream.

Cover the gelatine with cold water; when softened add the boiling water and stir until dissolved; add the strawberry juice, lemon juice and salt; set away to cool until it begins to thicken; whip the eggs until stiff; add two tablespoonfuls of sugar and beat together; when the gelatine is slightly thickened beat with Dover egg-beater until light; add the whites of the eggs, and lastly the whipped cream: dip the mould in cold water and drain; fill with the mixture and set away to harden; do not use a tin mould; pineapple, grape, lemon, orange, currant, raspberries, cherry, etc., may be used in place of strawberry: cut in slices and serve with cake.

FIG PUDDING.

One-third box of gelatine,
One-third cupful of cold water,
One-third cupful of boiling water,
Juice of one orange with water enough added to make one and one-third cupfuls,

One cupful of sugar.
White of one egg,
One pint of whipped cream,
One-half pound of figs,
Juice of half a lemon.

Cover the gelatine with cold water and let stand until soft; cook the sugar and hot water to a syrup; pour the boiling syrup over the gelatine and stir until dissolved; strain and cool; whip the egg; add cream to egg and stand the bowl in a pan of ice water; add the gelatine mixture and stir until it thickens; chop the figs and cover with the lemon juice; let stand while making the pudding; add figs to the pudding, and let stand on the ice until thickened.

PEACHES IN JELLY.

One-third box of gelatine,
One-third cupful of cold water,
One-third cupful of boiling water,

One-third cupful of sugar,
One and one-third cupfuls of peach liquid and water,
Few drops of almond extract.

Cut the peaches in slices; cover the gelatine with cold water and let soak until soft; cook the sugar with the boiling water and pour the hot syrup over the softened gelatine; strain and add the peach liquor and water, then the extract; let stand until it begins to thicken; peel and slice the peaches; put into a mould; pour the slightly thickened gelatine over the peaches and set on ice until it thickens; serve with whipped cream.

GINGER CREAM.

One-third box of gelatine,
One-half cupful of cold water,
One-half cupful of boiling water,
One cupful of powdered sugar,

One-fourth pound of crystallized ginger,
One pint of whipped cream,
Whites of two eggs.

Soak the gelatine in cold water until soft; add the boiling water and stir until dissolved; let stand until cold; whip the whites of the eggs until stiff; add the whipped cream; place the bowl in a pan of ice water; sift in the sugar; then add the gelatine and mix lightly; when thickening add the ginger, chopped fine and mixed with a little powdered sugar; dip an ice cream brick in cold water and drain; fill with the cream and let stand until thickened; cut in slices when serving.

CHARLOTTE RUSSE.

Three pints of whipped cream,
One tablespoonful of gelatine,

One-half cupful of powdered sugar,
One teaspoonful of vanilla.

Measure the cream after it is whipped; cover the gelatine with cold water and let stand until soft; add one-third of a cupful of boiling

water, stirring until dissolved; when cold strain into the cream carefully, stirring all the time to prevent lumping; add the vanilla and stir
until it thickens; line the cases or a glass dish with lady fingers; fill
with the cream and set on ice until serving time.

BAVARIAN CREAM.

One-third box of gelatine,   One and one-half cupfuls of milk,
One-half cupful of cold water,   Eight tablespoonfuls of whipped
Whites of three eggs,   cream.

Soak the gelatine in cold water until soft; scald the milk; pour the
hot milk over the softened gelatine; whip the cream; whip the whites
of the eggs to a stiff froth; add the sugar and beat together; set the
bowl into ice water; stir the gelatine until it begins to thicken; add the
beaten white of the egg, the cream and vanilla; stir until thickened;
the gelatine will thicken very quickly after it begins, so the cream and
egg must be added instantly; if the gelatine becomes too thick to mix
smoothly set the bowl in a pan of hot water and stir until it liquifies,
then add the cream and egg; mould; serve with cake.

SNOW PUDDING.

One-fourth of a box of gelatine,   One half cupful of boiling water,
One cupful of sugar,   Juice of one lemon with water
Whites of three eggs,   enough added to make three-
One-half cupful of cold water,   fourths of a cupful.

Cover the gelatine with the cold water and let soak until soft; add
the boiling water and stir until it dissolves; beat the whites of the eggs
stiff; add the sugar and beat together; add the lemon juice and water
to the gelatine and let stand until cold; set the bowl into a pan of ice
water; when it begins to thicken beat with Dover egg-beater until
light; add the beaten white of the egg and beat until thickened; pour
into a glass dish and set on the ice to harden; never mould food which
contains acid in tin; serve the pudding with a custard sauce made from
the yolks of the eggs; three tablespoonfuls of sugar; one pint of milk;
one teaspoonful of vanilla, one-half saltspoonful of salt; scald the milk;
beat the eggs until creamy; add the sugar and beat together; pour the
hot milk over the beaten egg and stir over the fire until creamy; when
cold add the vanilla.

WINE JELLY.

One box of gelatine.   One cupful of cold water,
Three cupfuls of boiling water,   One pint of sherry,
One pint of sugar,   Juice of one lemon.

Cover the gelatine with the cold water and let stand until softened;
add the boiling water and stir until dissolved; cook the sugar in one
cupful of water five minutes; strain the gelatine into the syrup; add
the wine and lemon juice; strain through a napkin and set on ice for
six or eight hours. Orange, lemon, grape or any fruit jelly may
be made in this way.

❀ Sherbets ^{and} Ice Cream ❀

DIRECTIONS FOR FREEZING.

Pour the mixture into the tin can; put the beater in and put on the cover; put the can into the tub and see that the point on the bottom of the can fits into the socket in the tub; put on the crosspiece and turn to see if everything is in place; break the ice very fine; put a layer of about four inches in the bottom of the tub, and then a layer of salt, using about three times as much ice as salt; put on another layer of ice and one of salt, and continue until the tub is full; turn the crank slowly until the cream begins to harden then turn rapidly for about ten minutes. It will be hard to turn when the mixture is frozen; wipe the salt and water from the cover; turn back the crosspiece and take off the cover without displacing the can; remove the beater and scrape the cream from it; pack the cream down; cover and cork the hole; put on the crosspiece and pack the ice tightly, adding more ice and salt; let stand two or three hours to ripen. To mould cream, fill the mould, pressing the cream into every corner; cover, seal by wrapping a piece of muslin, dipped in softened fat, around the mould where the cover and mould join; pack in ice and salt for an hour; cover the bucket with an old rug or piece of carpet. This prevent the ice melting rapidly.

BRICK ICE CREAM.

Freeze the cream without any flavoring; when frozen remove the dasher; set a bowl in a pan of ice water; take about a pint of the frozen cream; mix it until it is creamy; add the flavoring desired; mix thoroughly and place in the bottom of the mould; mix another portion of the frozen cream with a second flavoring and spread it on top; continue until the mould is filled; seal and pack in ice and salt for an hour or more. To remove it from the mould dip into pan of boiling water; remove instantly and turn out the cream; or wrap the mould in a towel dipped in hot water; cut in slices to serve.

VANILLA ICE CREAM.

One pint of cream,
One cup of sugar,
Pinch of salt,

One-half cupful of water,
Two teaspoonfuls of vanilla.

Cook the sugar in the water for five minutes; add to the cream; add the vanilla; let cool and freeze.

CARAMEL ICE CREAM.

One pint of cream,
One-fourth cupful of water,

A cupful and a half of caramelized
sugar.

Boil one cupful of sugar with the water, without stirring, until it begins to brown; then stir until a golden brown in color; add one-half cupful of water and stir until dissolved. To the cream add the salt and caramelized sugar and freeze.

STRAWBERRY ICE CREAM.

One quart of berries,
Two cupfuls of sugar,

Half a saltspoonful of salt,
Three pints of cream.

Wash the berries; add one cupful of sugar and the salt and let stand; cook the other cup of sugar in half a cupful of water for five minutes; add the syrup to the cream; freeze the cream; when nearly frozen wipe off the cover carefully and add the crushed fruit; mixing it thoroughly with the cream; finish freezing and pack.

NEAPOLITAN ICE CREAM.

One quart of cream,
One quart of milk,
Six eggs,

Two cupfuls of sugar,
One-half saltspoonful of salt,
Two tablespoonfuls of flavoring.

Beat the eggs until creamy; add the salt; cook the sugar in a half cupful of water for five minutes; scald the milk; add the syrup and pour the hot milk over the beaten egg; cook over boiling water until creamy, but not curdled; when cool add the cream and flavoring; freeze.

The addition of one tablespoonful of gelatine, softened with a little cold water and dissolved in the hot milk, makes the cream smoother and richer.

NUT ICE CREAM.

Almonds, walnuts, cocoanut or pistachio nuts, blanched and chopped fine or pounded to a paste may be added to any of the recipes for ice cream. Allow one pint of nuts to each quart of cream.

MOOSE.

One quart of whipped cream,
Three teaspoonfuls of vanilla,

One and one-half cupfuls of powdered
sugar.

Whip the cream stiff; drain; add the vanilla and sift in the sugar.

Line ice cream mould with white paper; pour in the mixture; cover and seal the cover by dipping a piece of muslin, about one inch in width, into softened fat or grease; draw it tightly around the mould where the cover joins; fasten; pack the mould in a pail of ice and salt, using three times as much ice as salt; cover the pail with an old rug or blanket; let stand five or six hours; when taken from the ice and salt dip quickly into a pan of boiling water or wrap in a towel dipped in hot water; turn out the moose; cut in slices and serve with cake.

NESSELRODE PUDDING.

One pint of chestnuts,	One pint of sugar,
One pint of boiling water,	One pound of French candies,
One pint of almonds,	One pint of cream,
Yolks of six eggs,	One pint of pineapple.
One tablespoonful of vanilla,	

Shell, blanch and boil the chestnuts twenty minutes, or until soft; mash and rub through a sieve; blanch the almonds; chop fine and pound to a paste; boil the sugar and water together fifteen minutes; beat the yolks of the eggs until light; add to it the syrup; return to the fire and cook until it thickens; beat until cold; add the chestnuts, fruit, candies, almonds and vanilla, and freeze; pack and let stand two or three hours to ripen.

To blanch almonds or chestnuts, shell the nuts and pour boiling water over them; let stand two or three minutes; then throw them into cold water; remove the skins.

TO WHIP CREAM.

Very thick or very thin cream will not whip; the former will turn to butter and the latter will make a liquid froth.

Cream that will hardly pour should be deluted with equal quantity of milk before whipping. The cream should be icy cold. If you have not a whipping churn the simplest way to whip cream is to pour into a deep bowl; set in ice water and beat with a Dover egg-beater.

PINEAPPLE SHERBET.

One tablespoonful of gelatine,	One pint of water,
One pint can of pineapple,	Juice of one lemon.
One pint of sugar,	

Boil the sugar in a half cupful of water five minutes; cover the gelatine with cold water and let stand until softened; pour the hot syrup over the softened gelatine and stir until dissolved; to the pineapple add the pint of water and juice of the lemon; strain the dissolved gelatine into the mixture and freeze.

The whites of three eggs may be substituted in place of the gelatine, if desired. Any fruit juice may be substituted in place of pineapple.

LEMON ICE.

One quart of water,	Two cupfuls of sugar.
Juice of six lemons,	

Cook the sugar in one cupful of water five minutes; add the quart of water and lemon juice and freeze.

FRAPPÉ.

Freeze a fruit ice to a mush and serve in sherbet glasses.

❋ Beverages ❋

COFFEE.

A mixture of one-third Mocha and two-thirds Java makes the best coffee; the Mocha is used for flavor and the Java for strength. Coffee, if bought ground, should be kept in an air-tight can; if left open it will lose much of its delicious flavor.

Coffee should not be boiled longer than one or two minutes; when coffee is boiled for a long time we lose from our beverage the delicious aroma which permeates the room, leaving the coffee bitter. Allow one tablespoonful of coffee, for each cupful.

Four tablespoonfuls of finely ground coffee,	One egg white, or two egg shells, Two cupfuls of boiling water.
Two cupfuls of cold water,	

Have the coffee ground very fine (not pulverized); mix the dry coffee with the egg white; add the cold water and mix thoroughly; let come to the boiling point, slowly; boil one or two minutes; then add the boiling water and set on the back part of the stove where it will keep hot, but will not boil, for fifteen or twenty minutes; serve with hot milk and cream. Do not boil, simply scald the milk; boiled milk gives an unpleasant flavor. The egg is used to clear the coffee.

VIENNA COFFEE.

To one-fourth of a cupful of hot milk add two tablespoonfuls of whipped cream; fill the cup with hot coffee.

CHOCOLATE.

Scrape fine an ounce and a half of chocolate; put into a saucepan with one tablespoonful of water; cook until smooth; add to it one quart of scalding hot milk; mix thoroughly and serve with whipped cream. If unsweetened chocolate is used add two tablespoonfuls of sugar. If chocolate is allowed to boil it becomes oily.

TEA.

In making tea an earthen teapot is best; fill the teapot with boiling water and let stand five minutes; empty, and put in the tea; allowing one teaspoonful for each cupful; cover with freshly boiled water and allow it to stand on the stove where it will keep hot, but will not boil, for five minutes.

LEMONADE.

Juice of three and grated rind of one large lemon,	Half a cupful of sugar, Four cupfuls of water.

Cook the sugar and grated rind of the lemon in half a cupful of water for five minutes; let cool; squeeze the lemons; add the syrup and the remainder of the water; strain and serve ice cold.

—EAT—
...SWEET SEMOLA...

A peculiarly dainty and delicate dish for breakfast; also excellent for pudding or pancakes, and unequaled for breading fish or cutlets.

◎

USE
...MORNING MEAL...

for your morning meal. A most nutritious food, delightful to the palate and satisfying to the appetite. A favorite porridge (mush) for children.

◎

...PERFECTION PASTRY FLOUR...

Made especially for pastry. No ordinary bread flour will make pastry that will compare with the pastry made from this flour. Do you want nice cake, short pie crust, or puffy, flaky yeast powder biscuits? Use this flour. We do not recommend it for bread. No flour can be the best for both pastry and bread. For pastry this flour is perfection.

DEL MONTE
MILLING CO.,
SAN FRANCISCO, CAL.

PASTRY FLOUR

...CREAM FLAKE OATS...

The name is very appropriate. They are just like flakes of rich cream. If you like oats (and most people do) you can depend on having a treat when you eat Cream Flake Oats.

◎——

...DEL MONTE SELF-RAISING BUCKWHEAT...

Prepared from the choicest grain and materials. It makes a lighter cake, and the cakes have more of the buckwheat flavor than can be obtained from any other preparation in the market. Don't take our word, but try it.